WALKING
THE
WAY
OF
LOVE

WALKING
THE
WAY
OF
LOVE

Edited by Courtney Cowart

CHURCH
PUBLISHING
INCORPORATED

Church Publishing
19 East 34th Street
New York, NY 10016
www.churchpublishing.org

Cover design by Jennifer Kopec, 2Pug Design
Typeset by PerfecType, Nashville, Tennessee

A record of this book is available from the Library of Congress.
ISBN-13: 978-1-64065-296-5 (paperback)
ISBN-13: 978-1-64065-297-2 (ebook)

Contents

Foreword

Michael B. Curry

Jesus said: "Abide in me as I abide in you. Just as the branch cannot bear fruit by itself unless it abides in the vine, neither can you unless you abide in me. I am the vine, you are the branches. Those who abide in me and I in them bear much fruit, because apart from me you can do nothing. . . . As the Father has loved me, so I have loved you; abide in my love. If you keep my commandments, you will abide in my love, just as I have kept my Father's commandments and abide in his love. I have said these things to you so that my joy may be in you, and that your joy may be complete."

—John 15:4–5, 9–11

Charles Marsh of the University of Virginia once observed that "Jesus had founded the most revolutionary movement in human history: a movement built on the unconditional love of God for the world and the mandate to live that love."[1]

---

1. Charles Marsh, *The Beloved Community: How Faith Shapes Social Justice from the Civil Rights Movement to Today* (New York: Perseus Books, 2005), 81.

This is true. Jesus of Nazareth began the most profoundly revolutionary movement in history. It was a movement of people for whom this Jesus, his teaching, his example, his risen life became the epicenter of their lives, and his way of love became their way of life. As a result, their lives were changed, and they changed the world around them.

It was two years ago that I asked a group of wise leaders to sit with me and discern together just how to help our beloved Episcopal Church to grow spiritually awake and more centered on this Jesus. At the time, I explained that in my first few years as presiding bishop, I had been traveling the church encouraging us to become more than just the Episcopal Church. We are not simply or even primarily a religious organization. We are in our origins, our roots, our soul, the Episcopal branch of the Jesus Movement. Jesus said, "I am the vine, you are the branches." Together we wondered: how can we practically help each other, as twenty-first-century followers of Jesus, to live as those branches of his movement and recapture the vitality of the first-century Jesus Movement that changed lives and their known world?

I am convinced that the Spirit lead us to a clear answer: follow Jesus and his way of love. It was the key in the first century, and it is the key in our time.

The chapters that follow are reflections on Jesus and his way of love, written by members of that circle of leaders and scholars who gathered around me for that important conversation, along with those who greatly influenced us. I am deeply grateful to them all.

We were united at that time, and remain so, in our desire to help our church to make a major culture shift. We knew just how much was at stake, for us as a church and for the whole Christian family.

The popular image of Christianity has grown moribund. We have seen and mourned the capitulation of Christianity to selfish, self-centered instincts. How could Christians care so little about the poor? How could Christians defend racism and white supremacy? When did we sell our soul? I thought two years ago and am more convinced than ever that we need a Christianity that looks like Jesus: a countercultural Christianity, counter even to the culture of popular Christianity itself. We need to knit the social gospel and evangelical gospel back together, because they are actually the same gospel.

That is my prayer, not just for us in the Episcopal Church but for all of Christianity in the West that we could recenter our lives on Jesus of Nazareth. Because the record of history is clear: the further we Christians have gone from Jesus, his teachings, his example, his risen life, the more likely it is that we will follow our own selfish path, oppress and hurt others, and quote everything but Jesus. For the church to be the church, we have to start with Jesus of Nazareth. His life, his teachings, his love of God, and his unselfish way of moving about the world—on Christ the solid rock we stand; all other ground truly is sinking sand.

The Way of Love helps us to abide close to Jesus, doing what he did, living how he lived. It helps us to look and live more like the Jesus Movement, that daring community of people who follow Jesus into loving, liberating, life-giving relationship with God, each other, and the whole of God's creation—a community of people who know that life with Jesus changes lives and changes the world. That is my prayer for the whole church.

I also pray for every individual Episcopalian and every Episcopal congregation. So many Episcopalians don't know if we have a relationship with God. We quietly wonder, "Am I really loved by God?" In absence of that love, or a deep awareness of that love, we just keep doing what we're doing. But we don't have to leave each other there. We could have so much more.

We could follow the advice of Dietrich Bonhoeffer and *throw ourselves into the arms of God*. I remember sharing his exhortation as part of my General Convention sermon in 2018, when we rolled out the Way of Love. Bonhoeffer saw people getting all twisted up in his day, trying to figure out how to follow Jesus's commandments, give up possessions, love their enemies, do all these impossible things. He warned them not to approach it as if it's mechanical and legalistic.

Instead, he said, "Throw yourself completely into the arms of God."[2] Turn around and throw yourself into Jesus's waiting arms. Then you might actually learn to love your enemy. Then you might pray, even for those who curse you. Then you will read Scripture and love the God you meet there. Then you will worship in Spirit and in truth. Then you will know what it means to bless and be blessed. Then you will go to the highways and byways with our Lord and make his ministry of reconciliation your own. Then you will rest in the arms of God and know nothing you have done was in vain.

---

2. Dietrich Bonhoeffer, *Letters and Papers from Prison*, vol. 8, *Dietrich Bonhoeffer Works,* ed. Eberhard Bethge (Minneapolis: Fortress Press, 209), 482, paraphrased by Presiding Bishop Michael B. Curry, sermon at the opening Eucharist of the 79th General Convention. Austin, TX, July 5, 2018.

When we walk along Jesus's Way of Love, we aren't simply walking. We're abiding with him, moving toward him, leaning into him. We are, in Bonhoeffer's words, throwing ourselves completely into his arms. We are forming and re-forming communities that practice his way and abide in him with freedom and abandon. If it sounds terrifying, I suppose it is. That is why we walk together. Jesus needed company so he could devote his life to his Father's purpose. And so do we!

So I am not praying that we will ordain more clergy or construct more buildings. That's not going to change the church or save the world. I pray that every Episcopalian would take a deep breath and leap into intimate relationship with Jesus. Make his Way of Love or some similar set of intentional Christian practices your own way of life, and find a community of people who share that commitment. Then you can walk together and not grow weary. Then his joy will be in us, and our joy will be complete.

An Invitation to Walk the Way of Love

Courtney Cowart

The other day a friend in New York took me to meet James Kim, a gifted spiritual guide to people of all generations. As we were visiting, I made a remark to Kim about being a mentor and spiritual teacher, but he immediately rejected that label. "I am not a teacher. I am not a guru," he said. "I am simply a reminder."

As I began to edit the chapters of this book, Kim's comment came back to me. On many levels, these reflections on the seven practices of the Way of Love are reminders. For some, they are reminders of truths from a lifetime of spiritual experience treasured deep in our hearts. For many of us, these will be reminders of good intentions and unsatisfied spiritual yearnings. For others, these are reminders of hopeful and inspiring recent events in the life of the Episcopal Church.

When Bishop Curry opened the 74th General Convention of the Episcopal Church in Austin, Texas, in July 2018, he asked each of us to commit more deeply to our journeys as disciples by engaging the ancient practices of the Way of Love.

That July the presiding bishop started with his own reminder: a passage from the Gospel of John, when Jesus turns to his disciples at the Last Supper and says, "As the Father has loved me so have I loved you. Now abide in my love." Bishop Curry continued:

> When [Jesus] knew their world would fall apart, when he knew uncertainty and ambiguity was in the air, when he knew that he did not know for sure, or precisely, what lay ahead, and all he could do was trust the Father, and leave it in the Father's hands. . . . [I]t is then that he said to them what he may be saying to us, "I am the vine, you are the branches. I am the vine, you are the branches. Abide in me and I in you, . . . for apart from me you can do nothing. But abide in me and you will bear much fruit, and so prove to be my disciples."[1]

In that moment, the presiding bishop gave us Jesus's definition of a disciple: one who practices abiding in Jesus's love.

Then Bishop Curry asked another question: how do we abide in Jesus's love? To answer that question, he referenced the text you just read in his foreword, the words of Dietrich Bonhoeffer in *The Cost of Discipleship*, who warned if you approach relationship with Jesus in a

---

1. Presiding Bishop Michael B. Curry, sermon at the opening Eucharist of the 79th General Convention. Austin, TX, July 5, 2018.

mechanical, legalistic way, you'll stumble. The way to really live into being a disciple, the way to abide in Jesus's love, is to throw yourself completely into the arms of the living God.

Archbishop Rowan Williams made much the same point in his enthronement sermon as the 104th archbishop of Canterbury when he reminded us, "We do not solve our problems with better discipline. What we need is better discipleship." The journey is about passionate relationship, he said, "entering into the intimate joy of Jesus's life," "moving into the radiant mystery of Christ." He continued:

> This is the opposite of treating the mystery of Jesus as something we can think about at arms' length, as an interesting phenomenon that has nothing really to do with how we live and die. In Matthew 11, Jesus rounds on those who do and says in essence, "I don't want your idle curiosity or I don't want your patronage. There is a secret that you haven't a clue about—and the ones who know that secret are the ones who don't try to protect themselves by staying at a safe distance."[2]

Instead, they throw themselves into the arms of the living God; hurl their lives into the hands of Jesus. Archbishop Rowan concluded by suggesting who models this Way for us:

---

2. Rowan Williams, sermon preached at his enthronement as the 104th archbishop of Canterbury, Canterbury Cathedral, February 27, 2003.

[I]t's time for you to listen to those who know their need. For them God is immediate—not an idea, not a theory, but life, food, air. . . . We can't know fully who God is and what God gives unless we are willing to abide—to stand in the same place as Jesus, in the full flood of the divine life poured out in mercy and renewal. It's only in the water that you can begin to swim.[3]

Throughout the chapters of this book you will hear many descriptions of where Jesus abides for those who know their need, and how we can seek through practice to join him in the flood of divine life, receiving mercy and renewal. We are all invited to dive into this water and swim.

Each contributor to this book shares a passionate conviction that it is time to remember, or perhaps to discover for the first time, how spiritual practice leads us into this experiential relationship with Jesus. While each chapter takes a unique approach to the topic of a given practice, all are clearly writing from an experience and witness of God's immediacy in the context of Christian life and practice. We are all walking together, and our lives are changed because of that commitment.

A Common Journey

The contributors also hold in common a more specific journey: our offerings began to take shape in retreat with Presiding Bishop Curry

---

3. Ibid.

in December 2017. It was in retreat together that we articulated for the first time as a group why engaging Jesus's practices as individuals and as a church matters, and how Christian spiritual practices are linked to reinvigorating our collective relationship with God. Those insights and hopes shape much of what you will read in the pages that follow.

When we gathered in Atlanta, we recognized the great challenge before us: the decline of the church in the United States is in part due to our failure to help people make spiritual meaning of their lives. Some of the struggle is simply the age in which we live. As scholar and priest Dwight Zscheile admits in his chapter on the practice of Learn, "In a secular age, it is very difficult for people to imagine and be led by the power and presence of God."

However, for that very reason, as Bishop Robert Wright reminds us in his chapter on the practice of *Go*, our witness today matters perhaps more than ever. In a time when Christianity is countercultural, and deep, faithful discipleship in a secular context is more challenging, "[w]e are here in this millennium, this century, this decade, this year, month and day because we are *supposed* to be here. . . . [W]e are also the people suited to help God turn the world right-side-up by following Jesus now." We have been chosen for such a time as this.

While this recognition of our calling as disciples bestows great dignity and purpose, it can also feel daunting. As priest and spiritual leader Jesús Reyes names in his chapter on creating a *Rule of Life*, our commitments to grow in faithfulness and deepen our relationship with God do not depend on our efforts only; rather, all our efforts are saturated in grace. As is often said, there is a reason we call these *practices*. Br. David Vryhof of the Society of St. John the Evangelist reassures us in his chapter on *Pray* that prayer is God's gift to us, not a duty or a chore, and that we may rest assured "God appreciates all our attempts."

As much as the Way of Love provides a way for us to reclaim Christian voice and witness, it is also a way for us to make an interior return to God and to find stillness in the presence of God as a way to discover our deepest moral alignment and integrity. Scholar and sociologist Catherine Meeks names this gift in her chapter on the practice of *Turn*. "There must be a way for the followers of Jesus today to find our own deep connections to the divine. We can come to understand the inner community that lives in our hearts and minds, so that we are more free to listen to the same still, small voice of God that spoke to the prophet Elisha."

Indeed, there is a way. It is Jesus's Way of Love. In Frank Logue's chapter on *Worship,* we see how all the practices come together to lead us to our home in God. "[I]n worship we turn, learn, and pray as a gathered body and so are empowered to bless and go before we pause once more, finding our rest in God alone."

Preparing to Walk

The other day I was reading a little book by the Jewish mystic Martin Buber, titled *The Way of Man.* Buber writes about the first practice

Christianity shares with Judaism, which we have called *Turn*. To turn, Buber says, we must become the ones who search our hearts and come to say, like Adam, in and before God, "I hid myself."[4] As a first step, we must admit that.

Then, in that context and with that admission and self-reminder before God, the spiritual practices of prayer and worship, the study of Scripture, reaching out to bless our neighbor, going to meet and embrace the stranger, each in different ways make us vulnerable, remind us of our need, keep our hearts open, and cause us to keep reaching for God. This is how the practices begin to awaken us and destroy the various systems we devise to hide out from God. The practices that strip our illusions are essential, because, as Buber teaches, "If we drown the Voice of God or hide from the face of God, our life will never become a *way*."[5]

If we do turn and we do begin to emerge from hiding, the Way of Love practices have the power to wake us up spiritually each and every day. They are transformative if we engage them with the intention to expose our lives to God's gentle recreation of us through them, as we pray each reader will.

If there is another spiritual giant whose influence and inspiration is woven through the chapters of this book, it is the great mystic and mentor of Martin Luther King Jr., Howard Thurman. More than

---

4. Martin Buber, *The Way of Man*, Book IV: *Hasidism and Modern Man* (1958; Amherst, NY: Humanity Books, 2000), 126.
5. Ibid.

one of the contributors reference him prominently, and I suspect his wisdom was in the hearts of many more as we wrote. Many of us who have worked on the Way of Love consider him one of our greatest influences.

In the vocational discernment work I have done with communities, congregations, and individuals over the past fourteen years, one of my favorite centering reflections draws on Thurman's wisdom. It has proven almost foolproof in helping all sorts of people learn how not to drown out the Voice of God.

The practice is very simple: we read the passage below and then divide into triads to engage storytelling. We do what several of the authors you will read strongly advocate, and that is to take the time to listen deeply to one another's stories about times when we heard the Voice of God, or as Thurman calls it, the "Sound of the Genuine." We also create space for people to share stories of times we hid from that voice. This can indeed be a threshold practice as one begins to transform one's "life" into Jesus's "way."

In closing, I invite you to close your eyes, center yourself in the presence of God, and pause for just a minute to dedicate yourself to this journey of practice, listening for sound of the Voice of God. Drop your attention from your head down into your heart, breathe into that space and feel it opening. Then ask God to enter and show you God's abiding presence already within you.

Here are Howard Thurman's profound words, which encapsulate the purpose of each practice you will dwell with along the Way of Love. Consider his words a kind of prelude and summary of our prayer for you and for all of us on the path Jesus walked first:

There is in every person something that waits and listens for the sound of the genuine in herself [or himself]. . . . There is in you something that waits and listens for the sound of the genuine in yourself. Nobody like you has ever been born and no one like you will ever be born again—you are the only one. . . .

If you cannot hear it, you will never find whatever it is for which you are searching. . . . If you cannot hear the sound of the genuine in you, you will all of your life spend your days on the ends of strings that somebody else pulls. . . .

The sound of the genuine is flowing through you. Don't be deceived and thrown off by all the noises that are a part even of your dreams, your ambitions that you don't hear the sound of the genuine in you. Because that is the only true guide that you will ever have and if you don't have that you don't have a thing.[6]

May you listen and hear the Voice of God—the sound of the genuine—flowing through you every moment. When you turn and study sacred texts, when you pray and worship, when you bless others and engage the stranger, when you take times of rest and return to the journey—in all that you say and do, may you listen for the One who accompanies you.

And know this: we also walk with you.

---

6. Howard Thurman, "The Sound of the Genuine," baccalaureate address at Spelman College, Atlanta, GA, May 4, 1980.

CHAPTER 1

Reflections on a Rule of Life

Jesús Reyes

Self-care is never a selfish act—it is simply good stewardship of the only gift I have, the gift I was put on earth to offer others. Anytime we can listen to true self and give the care it requires, we do it not only for ourselves, but for the many others whose lives we touch.

—Parker Palmer, *Let Your Life Speak: Listening for the Voice of Vocation*

I, wisdom, live with prudence,
and I attain knowledge and discretion.

—Proverbs 8:12

The Way of Love is an intentional commitment to a set of spiritual practices that shape and center us in the life of Jesus.

Many would call it a "rule of life," a phrase that may conjure fear, anxiety, images of rigidity, or memories of working hard to please an angry God and coming up short. Let us dispel that notion from the beginning. Engaging the Way of Love or any rule of life begins not with rules, but with a yearning to follow in the pathway of Jesus and with a trust in God's abiding grace.

So imagine that we are simply here, invited as we are: people who have hopes and dreams, searching for a solid spiritual grounding. The first step in this journey is to open ourselves to God's grace.

Grace is the unconditional and abiding presence of God within and around us. It operates in us, inspiring and transforming our human tendencies, making it possible for us to bear fruit in lives dedicated back to God.

Never assume, though, that grace is easy. It can be disorienting and messy. Undeniably, when we are moved by grace, we are bound to reach beyond our wildest imagination. Grace draws us into our truest selves. It calls us to take bold steps and loving risks. Grace is the nudge that sends us into prayer. Grace strengthens us when we feel vulnerable, so we can keep moving, keep loving, and keep growing into maturity in Christ.

This is what we call in our Christian tradition being "sanctified." You may be familiar with the hymn "Amazing Grace" by John Newton, an English poet and cleric. It is an articulation of the transformative experience the Way of Love invites you to enter deeply.

Amazing grace! how sweet the sound,
That saved a wretch like me!

I once was lost, but now am found,
    Was blind, but now I see.

'Twas grace that taught my heart to fear,
    And grace my fears relieved;
How precious did that grace appear
    The hour I first believed! . . .

The Lord hath promised good to me,
    His word my hope secures;
He will my shield and portion be
    As long as life endures.[1]

As we begin, you can assert with confidence that God's grace is a given. We do not have to labor for it, but we do have to recognize it, receive it, and learn to share it. As we read in 2 Corinthians, "[Jesus said,] 'My grace is sufficient for you, for power is made perfect in weakness.' So, I will boast all the more gladly of my weaknesses, so that the power of Christ may dwell in me" (2 Cor. 12:9).

Grace cannot be stored. It is not a transactional commodity. Grace is free and it is freeing from self-centeredness. We share it with others just by living in it. Community is made stronger when we share the grace that is already in us. Grace is the cornerstone of the Way of Love we live together.

---

1. John Newton, "Amazing grace! How sweet the sound," in *A Collection of Sacred Ballads,* compiled by Richard Broaddus and Andrew Broaddus, 1790.

What Is a Rule of Life?

A rule of life is an ancient pattern of spiritual practice rooted in the monastic and mystical Christian traditions. The best-known rule of all is the Rule of St. Benedict of Nursia, a sixth-century mystic. Monastic rules like Benedict's provided guiding principles to aid monks and nuns in their spiritual formation and to center them on the spiritual journey. In monastic contexts, a rule of life is prescribed. In other words, the person freely steps into an already defined system of practice and way of living.

Monastics aren't the only ones who benefit from a rule of life. For us, it is a personal commitment to live our lives in a specific and well-oriented way that forms us into the likeness of Jesus. A rule in this sense holds what you truly believe and makes those beliefs evident in your daily choices and actions. Your rule of life will be formulated through prayer, discernment, and openness to divine inspiration. Once developed, your rule of life will become a solid and reliable spiritual and moral compass. It will orient you, express who you are, and help you to remain authentic. Dedicated to it, you will look and live more like the one you were born to be and more like Jesus.

The Practice before the Practice: Learning to Listen

The first sentence of the preface of St. Benedict's Rule is a wise word for all of us. It reads, "Listen carefully, my son, to the master's instructions, and attend to them with the ears of your heart."[2] Although most of us are not monastics, we should treasure this teaching, because learning to listen with the ears of our heart to our own life and the lives of others is foundational for discerning a rule of life.

During my early teenage years, I joined a karate practice. My intent was to learn the art of throwing kicks and punches and receive the benefits of self-defense and exercise. What I discovered was something very different. Our dojo master did not begin by teaching us fighting techniques. He started by teaching us to breathe. Before we began to exercise, we needed to develop a sense of awareness and understanding of something as simple yet powerful as our own breath.

The dojo master always endeavored to help us develop the capacity to "listen to our bodies." We were taught: "The discipline of karate is the discipline of the self. Breathing is about developing your capacity to listen to your body, as it breathes, as it moves, and is stretched to its maximum potential." After this we started to learn the punching and kicking, but the foundation was the breathing. We began to exercise, but without losing the awareness of our own breathing. Now that I think of it, karate became one of my earliest spiritual practices. As I learned to pay attention to my breath, I learned to listen.

---

2. Benedict of Nursia, *The Rule of St. Benedict in English* (Collegeville, MN: Liturgical Press, 1982), 15.

Your rule of life is about the art of living. The art of living depends on your capacity to listen. As Parker Palmer explains, "Before I can tell my life what I want to do with it, I must listen to my life telling me who I am."[3] The beginning of the process of discerning a rule of life is to pay attention, breathe, and listen to your life. If you are quiet enough, pay attention, and listen deeply enough, you enter the space where your true self resides. Nobody else inhabits this private, sacred place: just you and God. It is the holiest of all spaces. It is the origin of the dignity of every human being. It is the spring of living waters Jesus describes for his disciples.

When we are discerning a rule of life, we want to step into this realm and drink from this fresh, living water. We want to craft a pattern of life that prioritizes living from this authentic and Jesus-centered place. To do that, we must learn to listen first using the "ears of our heart." Allow this to be the departing point as you formulate a personal rule of life.

Why Formulate a Rule of Life?

One of the most basic human aspirations is to find consistency and authenticity in life. The heart of the Benedictine spiritual tradition is centeredness. Finding the center in oneself is like identifying the

---

3. Parker Palmer, *Let Your Life Speak: Listening for the Voice of Vocation* (San Francisco: Jossey-Bass, 2000), 4.

compass's "jewel bearing," the point where the magnetic arrow rests. Being properly centered is essential for the maximal functioning of all the parts.

One might say a rule of life is your compass, and faith is the jewel bearing that keeps the whole instrument (your life) well-oriented and centered on Jesus. Imagine that your rule of life is the point of reference that will orient your life, each step of the way, back to Jesus and his way.

Spiritual centeredness, well-grounded personal identity, and harmonious existential clarity are just some of the fruits you may experience as you engage a rule of life focused on practicing Jesus's Way of Love. Think of these fruits as the "deliverables." As Paul writes in the fourth chapter of the letter to the Philippians:

> Rejoice in the Lord always; again I will say, Rejoice. Let your gentleness be known to everyone. The Lord is near. Do not worry about anything, but in everything by prayer and supplication with thanksgiving let your requests be made known to God. And the peace of God, which surpasses all understanding, will guard your hearts and your minds in Christ Jesus. (Phil. 4:4–7)

It's not helpful to think of this as transactional: if I practice this rule, then I get inner peace. But the fruits of a life in the Spirit are more likely to manifest when our lives are organized around a gracious, intentional rule that shapes us in the image of Jesus.

Formulating Your Rule of Life

The formulation of a rule of life involves two basic questions:

1. What is God calling me to be?
2. What is God calling me to do?

These two questions address the divine and human aspects of the self. As you formulate your rule, you will engage a conscious and faithful process of connecting these two dimensions of reality that are alive within you. In the process of discernment, you will seek to harmonize them.

Feel free to try this visualization exercise:

Locate yourself in the Vatican at the Sistine Chapel. If it would help you, search for some pictures of this famous chapel.

You are walking through the chapel, admiring Michelangelo's frescos. Pay attention to the ceiling and stop at the section known as *The Creation of Adam*. Adam is nude, reclining on the earth. God is being carried by a celestial community through the clouds. They are reaching toward each other.

Focus now on God and Adam's hands, especially on the fingers. There is amazing tension there. God's *ru'ach*—God's spirit, wind, energy, and life—is being transmitted into

Adam. This is an act of deep intimacy between God and humanity. At creation the Untouchable God becomes accessible to humanity.

Depicted in this image are two ways God has demonstrated God's love for us: the act of giving life and the act of becoming available to humanity. Imagine, as you reflect on your rule of life, that this is your personal spiritual experience. Instead of Adam, you are the one God is touching. You are the one receiving God's *ru'ach*.

As you gently come out of the visualization, ask yourself:

- What helps me to feel that God and I are touching?
- What does my life look like, when I am receiving God's *ru'ach*? What would I be saying and doing?

Another approach may be to imagine that through the formulation and practice of a rule of life, you are following in the footsteps of Nicodemus. In Jesus's encounter with him in John 3:1–15, Jesus tells Nicodemus, "Very truly, I tell you, no one can see the kingdom of God without being born from above" (John 3:3). Consider the formulation of your rule of life as a spiritual exercise, recognizing your own potential for spiritual rebirth, as you reflect on the questions: "What is God calling me to be?" and "What is God calling me to do?" Remember to breathe, to listen, and to move through this process in a state of prayer, meditation, and contemplation.

How Can I Formulate My Rule of Life?

Now you are ready for an exercise that, by God's grace, will help you to discover, adjust, and live into your own rule of life.

I like the combination of these three words: "discover, adjust, and live into." Consciously and/or unconsciously, we all are already following norms, laws, directives, and patterns that orient us toward whatever we understand as "normal." Norms help us to avoid error; at the same time, we do not want to just follow the path uncritically or unconsciously. It would be too easy for the individual, unduly guided by trends and social expectation, to fall into a state of domestication. And there is nothing domesticated about a life in the Spirit.

Formulating a personal rule of life is about asking deep, critical spiritual questions, and the journey this practice initiates will include discovery, adjustment, and living into new understandings of who you truly are. Part of the lifelong journey of discovering your God-given vocation and identity is slowly, sometimes painfully, but always graciously stripping away the habits that keep us from living as our true selves in Christ.

It has been said that we are always practicing something. My personal experience tells me that all of us are following a kind of rule of life. The question: have we unconsciously acquired this rule over the course of random life experience and development, or are our practices something we are aware of, can articulate and reflect upon, and use as a conscious point of reference for living from a true spiritual core?

Unless we intentionally create a rule of life, our lives can quickly become unclear, uncertain, and unmanageable. Put differently, our lives may fit norms the world has laid out, but we will not be any closer to God's intention for us.

Your Life, Centered in Jesus: A Rule of Life Exercise

This exercise will follow the four stages of Lectio Divina (*Lectio*/Reading, *Meditatio*/Meditation, *Oratio*/Prayer, *Contempletio*/Contemplation), plus an addition step: *Actio*/Action. Lectio Divina is an ancient monastic approach to reading the Holy Scriptures. In our case, we will use these stages to read our own life with the intent of recentering ourselves in Jesus.

First Stage—Reading

This stage is about reading your own life with intent and attention. It is about breaking the diverse facets of your life into very small pieces: what you think of yourself, what others think of you, and what you admire in others.

- First Step: write down five words, short phrases, descriptors, or human values, that speak of who you are.
- Second Step: write down five words, short phrases, descriptors, or human values others have used to describe you.
- Third Step: write down five words, short phrases, descriptors, or human values you have admired in others.

What I say of myself	What others say of me	What I admire in others
Reliable	*Kind to strangers*	*St. Paul's courage in the face of trials*
Generous	*Always does what he says*	*My mother's unconditional love*
A deep listener	*Wise*	*Sojourner Truth speaks truth to power*
Lover of God	*Thinks before speaking*	*Jesus's forgiveness*
Lives simply	*Joyous*	*My mentor's faithfulness to God*

Second Stage—Meditation

Mediating is about being attentive. So, remain in silence just listening to what you have written down. Allow these words and phrases to boil gently in your heart and in your mind. Take as much time as you want, then follow the recommended steps.

- First Step: as you go over each one of the fifteen words, short phrases, descriptors, or human values, pay attention to the words or values that repeat or are alike. Highlight them.
- Second Step: now select five words or values that you consider reflect your deepest motivations and aspirations in life.
- Third Step: match your word selections with the person of Jesus: something he said, something he did, a core value he held, or a story from the Gospels.

Second Step: My five chosen words/values	Third Step: Connection with Jesus
Truth and justice-seeker	I am the Truth; the truth will set you free. (John 14:6; 8:32)
Courageous	Don't be afraid. Just believe. (Mark 5:36)
Reliable and present	Jesus is the good shepherd (John 10:11); Jesus is with us until the very end. (Matt. 28:20)
Simple and generous	Those who lose their life for my sake will gain it. (Matt. 10:39)
Loving	Love God and love your neighbor as yourself. (Luke 10:27)

Third Stage—Prayer

Prayer is the act of the personal conversation we have with God. I want to stress the word "conversation," because it is not just about talking. It is about the mutual engagement that changes the two or more interacting agents. Consider the closeness of these two words "conversation" and "conversion." So, prayer is about the two elements put together: the act of conversing and growing in relationship with God, and the act of being converted to the likeness and ways of God.

- Formulate a prayer to God based on your five core values. Be creative in expressing what you have captured of yourself, your life aspirations, and how this vision is centered in Jesus. Keep the prayer simple and accessible to you.

- *This is your own summary of what a Jesus-centered life looks like for you.* Pray this prayer every day, as a way of asking God to fill and lead you toward this life.

- *Here is an example*: "Jesus, lover of souls, I receive with gratitude the gift of your presence in my life. Following in your footsteps, cloaked in your grace, may I speak and do only what is true and just this day. May I seek to give more and live simply, so that others might simply live. Make me steadfast and present, attentive and respectful to your presence in everyone and everything I encounter. In the face of fear, temptation, and hesitation, fill my heart with courage. Allow me to constantly breathe in your love, so that I can breathe out your love among friends, family, neighbors, enemies, and the world. I pray this in the name of Jesus and in the power of the Holy Spirit. Amen."

Fourth Stage—Contemplation

This is a daily exercise you do after you have prayed your prayer. At this stage, you venture into the future with the vision for Jesus-centered life you have created and contemplate what the day may bring. Pray about it, listen to God's still, small voice. Ask for the grace and gift to follow Jesus and live what you have prayed.

Fifth Stage—Action

In the Benedictine life, action occurs in the context of *Ora et Labora*, that is, Pray and Work. Both prayer and work are interwoven in a full life. This is the context where you live into your rule of life.

As you pray and act, notice how the practices of the Way of Love embody your summary of Jesus-shaped life. Notice how these practices prepare and nurture you for Jesus-shaped life. For instance, at the start or end of each day, you might pray with one or several of these questions:

- From what do you need to *turn* and what is God inviting you to turn toward, so you can live the Jesus-shaped life you have imagined for yourself? How could you actively, practically, and regularly check in with God about making that turn?
- How could *learning* and reading Scripture help you to live into one or more of the virtues that are for you part of Jesus-shaped life? When and how could you fold Scripture reading into each day?
- What is the role of *prayer* in a Jesus-shaped life for you? When and how could you build prayer into each day?
- Does *worship* grow any of the virtues you hope to embody as you live a Jesus-shaped life? When and how could you make worship more a part of your life?
- Which elements of your image of Jesus-shaped life would involve you *blessing* others with your story, resources, or presence . . . or receiving blessing from others?
- If God sent you to *go* across borders and beyond comfort, which of the virtues and values you've named would you need most? How could the practice of going actually grow this Jesus-shaped life in you?

- When you *rest*, does it help you to see your life more clearly? What experiences of rest make the most difference for you? How and when could you take intentional, prayerful rest and allow God to restore you for living the life God wants for you?

A Final Word on Living a Rule of Life

An important component of any faith journey is community. Recall the mystery of the Holy Trinity. God is a community: Father, Son, and Holy Spirit. We cannot possibly live as the people of God without similarly being rooted in a small, intentional community.

If your church or ministry has taken up the Way of Love, you could join an already existing small circle. If no such groups exist, take the initiative and form one made up of friends, family, people with whom you already serve in a ministry, or spiritually seeking neighbors. The Episcopal Church provides an accessible curriculum and video guide for creating a small group and practicing the Way of Love together. You will find it here: https://episcopalchurch.org/way-of-love/intentional-small-group-resources.

While the vision of Jesus-shaped life you have created is yours, you will travel further and deeper if you are surrounded by a small, intentional, practicing group of companions who are listening for God's call and following the way of Jesus too.

Once you have your rule of life and a community with which to live it, you can follow all the steps of the *Lectio Divina* cycle as you live it:

- Read your rule, God's word, and other holy words.
- Meditate and consider deeply what this wisdom is revealing and calling forth in your life.
- Pray your prayer for Jesus-centered life and add to it freely.
- Contemplate what is to come in your life.
- Action—bring all to life!

The spiritual discipline is to maintain your rule of life as a way of living, day after day, supported and surrounded by community, rooted in God's grace and love.

CHAPTER 2

Turn

Catherine Meeks

TURN: Pause, listen, and choose to follow Jesus

As [Jesus] was walking along, he saw Levi son of Alphaeus sitting at the tax booth, and he said to him, "Follow me." And he got up and followed him.

—Mark 2:14

Like the disciples, we are called by Jesus to follow the Way of Love. With God's help, we can turn from the powers of sin, hatred, fear, injustice, and oppression toward the way of truth, love, hope, justice, and freedom. In turning, we reorient our lives to Jesus Christ, falling in love again, again, and again.[1]

R epentance on a daily basis is a tough assignment for all of us. The first practice in the Way of Love is complex and difficult,

---

1. "Turn," Episcopal Church, https://episcopalchurch.org/way-of-love/practice/turn.

and yet it is foundational to transforming not only our lives but our world. It should come as no surprise that following the Way of Love seriously will require us to engage in daily acts of repentance and to pay careful attention to our inner lives. It is there that we will find the host of inner distractions that so often hinder our efforts to follow Jesus.

"Turning" is not a matter of simply asking God for help to do better. It is a matter of discovering what at our core is making it difficult for us to do better. Why do we do the opposite of what we have been taught and what we have told ourselves we want to do? This is not an easy question, and we are often too quick to rush to an overly simplified answer. It is crucial that we pray and ask God for help. But these petitions fall on rocky soil when they are not partnered with knowing what the internal battle is about in the first place.

Our churches can do more to help all of us engage in the inner healing work that must happen for us to be willing and able to turn to God wholeheartedly. They must teach us how to search for the sound of the genuine in ourselves, so that we will not be blown around by every wind that happens to pass us by. My most important mentor, Dr. Howard Thurman, teaches that one must always search for "the sound of the genuine" in himself or herself, and that one must look for what comprises our unique and absolute inner core in order to stand in the world in a way that is secure and that sustains our personhood.[2]

---

2. Howard Thurman, "The Sound of the Genuine," baccalaureate address at Spelman College, Atlanta, GA, May 4, 1980.

My deep appreciation for the importance of finding one's inner core prompts my approach to discussing what it means to "Turn." Much of what is required concerns human psychology, what I will call "the inner community," and a discussion of the shadow, persona, and projection.

The Core Questions

Who are you anyway? What are you seeking in this life? What do you care about? What do you live for? For what are you willing to die? This is not a series of mere academic questions. These are the questions that make it possible to turn and to go in a different direction in order to be true to your core.

As my colleague Jesús Reyes discussed in the previous chapter, when a person does not know what lies at their core, it is difficult for that person to make a worthwhile turn. There is little reason to engage in such actions as repentance and turning to a new way with God if it appears one direction is just as good as the next. The ability to turn to a new way of seeing must be rooted in the sense that such action matters at the depths of a person's soul. Such a reorientation is not simply a stand-alone activity that can easily be ignored. True turning is deeply rooted in the heart and head and grows out of deep awareness that comes from the depths.

This is why when you stand on the outside observing another person's life and behavior, it might seem a simple matter for that person to make a turn from one set of behaviors to more desirable or "holy" ones. But if you study the dynamics necessary to make a turn, it becomes clear that turning is a complicated matter that requires deep inner work. It is often a slow, invisible process.

Inherent in turning is repentance, which means to turn around or to change direction. How does one turn around? For many years, I have lamented the fact that the church mandates many good behaviors without making it clear how one is supposed to accomplish them. For instance, we are instructed to be forgiving, but there are few clear guides to help one understand that forgiveness is a process. So, what is involved in turning, toward Jesus or toward anything at all? How do we manage to turn? Is turning simply a matter of making up one's mind to be different? Let's spend time now exploring these questions and the challenges involved in the invitation to turn.

The Inner Community

Human beings are complicated entities, and all of us have many facets. Often, some of those facets are unknown even to us. In the world of psychology, we speak about these facets as an "inner community." In the first place, it is important to understand oneself as having such a community. Then it is critical to begin the process of working to engage that community in order to understand who occupies the inner space that helps to make you and your life.

There will be inner community members that are quite vocal about who they are. Think of these as the persona, or the way one presents one's self to the outer world. These are the characteristics that distinguish one person from another. For instance, we are seen as friendly, unfriendly, helpful, introverted, extraverted, kind, unkind, generous, stingy, self-assured, unsure of self, selfless, or self-centered, and the list could go on indefinitely. Everyone has a persona that the ego works very diligently to maintain.

But there is another feature in the inner community: the shadow. It contains those qualities that are harder to name. They are qualities that remain hidden just below the surface of consciousness, and yet they peek out many times during the day. They usually manifest themselves in the form of projection.

For example, the shadow is at work when we tell ourselves stories about something we have no information about. Perhaps you are driving and see a certain type of car and driver. You know nothing about this person, but you may begin to make judgments such as, "That doesn't look like the kind of person who should be driving such a car." You begin a conversation in your head about the driver, even though you have no information about the person. These types of conversations tell us a great deal about ourselves. You may concoct guesses about how the driver obtained the car. Perhaps you will even go so far as to decide the driver could not possibly own that car, because you believe that driver is not supposed to drive that car.

While this is a perfectly normal dynamic, it is quite dangerous. It is the dynamic that comes into play when police are profiling young men of color or when a physician decides against a course of treatment for a patient because the doctor has projected that the patient is too poor or not literate enough to carry out the plan. All projections are about the person who is making them. The conversation is in your head, with no concrete facts to support any of your conclusions.

This is the undeniable work of the shadow. These thoughts and feelings are generated out of parts of the inner community that even you are not conscious of. Projection like this does not have to be a serious problem, if the person making the projections recognizes what is happening and begins to stop it, realizing it is a story in their head and only in their head. As individuals begin to become more conscious and learn to integrate these thoughts and stories back into the rest of the inner community, there is a chance to learn something helpful and turn.

Projection becomes dangerous if a person holds onto the projection and insists upon it becoming reality. Oftentimes folks will insist their projections are true, even after meeting the person upon whom the projections were made. This refusal to withdraw projections in the face of facts to the contrary undergirds oppression and acts of inhumanity across the globe.

The Swiss psychiatrist Carl Jung believed if everyone would withdraw their shadow projections and own them as such, evil would be removed from the world.[3] While I do not quite agree with Jung—because I believe the negative energy of evil is a real entity that involves more than projections—I do believe we could interrupt evil and all manner of regrettable actions by withdrawing projections. This is especially important for people of faith who seek to live in the Way of Love that Jesus expended his life to demonstrate.

---

3. For example, Jung discusses the shadow and evil extensively in his autobiography, *Memories, Dreams, and Reflections*.

Working with the Shadow

What can we do about the shadow and its projections? The first and most important step is recognition and acceptance of its existence. Too many people seem to think our lives are being controlled by things that are external to us, as if someone else is causing whatever pain and distress we might experience. This has led to a surge in extraordinary rage around us, from mass shootings to dehumanizing language and other disrespectful acts. Imagine if instead we understood how our inner community bears upon the quality of our outer life.

If the only explanation for our daily struggles and ongoing well-being is assigned to forces outside of us, then as individuals we are relieved of any responsibility to do anything about our circumstances. Even worse, we give away our power to do anything about what is happening. When people give up their power by incorrectly assigning it to the wrong causes, rage and despair are close behind. Then it becomes easy to project onto a racial group, the government, or some individual or thing that must be responsible for our plight.

Perhaps one of the worst things that anyone can do is relinquish their personal power to a person or set of circumstances outside of themselves. People who view themselves as completely powerless are dangerous to themselves and others.

For this reason, it is vital that we understand that the persona we present to the world has a shadow. When you are being helpful and friendly, know that there is an opposite side, which means at times you can be unhelpful and unfriendly. When you identify with the positive side of yourself without taking into account the opposite side, it leads to hubris. Hubris is seeing yourself as more than you really are. Instead, pay attention to your opposites and become careful about focusing exclusively on the positive in your behavior. It can be a life-saving endeavor.

This does not mean that you need to go through life denigrating the self. I am speaking here of balance. Every person has many sides, and it is important to become self-aware about the many selves that live in your inner community. This is the first step in the work of confronting the shadow. And the confrontation with the shadow is the most crucial step in turning to a new way of seeing and doing. Turning is not as mysterious as it is often thought to be, but it definitely involves more than just making up your mind.

Knowledge Is Not Enough

It is often said that when people know better, they will do better, but that is not necessarily accurate. The ability to act in a different manner lies in the deep understanding of what is causing an action in the first place and what it takes to choose a different path. While self-knowledge is important, it is not simply a matter of knowing. If this were the case, our world would be in much better shape, because all of us know how to act much better than we manage to act on most days.

I recall how angry my first-year seminar students became when we studied the Holocaust. I proposed that they consider that each person in the room could have been a Nazi, because we had that capacity in our inner community. We were fortunate to live in a land where that energy was not activated, but that was as much a matter of historical circumstance as moral fortitude. My students did not like hearing this.

And yet, the ability to realize our capacity for the negative actually increases our capacity for the positive. With this honest awareness, we can pay attention and stay open to God's grace. This grace helps us to not be ruled by the negatives in our inner community.

When human beings remain unconscious about this dynamic, it leaves them at the mercy of the negative energy without knowing what is happening. Then that energy can orchestrate somewhat of an alternative life just below the surface of consciousness, a life that is capable of all types of disturbance. Raising it to the surface is necessary for healing energy to come alive in us, thus making it possible for us to turn toward new behaviors, thoughts, and feelings.

Managing the Shadow

Another way to manage shadow energy is to pay attention to the stories or the projections you make up throughout the day. When situations arise where you have no concrete information, but you find a story playing in your head, it is time to take a step back and own what is happening. The ego loves to fill in the blanks, even if the information is unfounded or completely false. Taking a step back and halting the untrue inner narrative will give you a moment to choose a better way.

Withdrawing that projection interrupts the negative thinking that could lead to hurtful action. If you think about what you were saying to yourself and ask why you created such a story, you can also learn something about yourself. Keeping a journal is a helpful tool for this kind of exploration. Regularly practicing this honest interrogation of self gets easier over time and eventually reduces the amount of projection you do each day.

Along with attending to projections, you might also pay attention to your nighttime dreams and learn even more about your inner community and what is hidden in the shadow side of your psyche. It may help to find a competent person who can assist in your dream work. With help and experience, you may find it simpler to understand what certain dream symbols mean.

Dreams are a viable way for listening to God.[4] One need only look at Holy Scripture, where plenty of prophets and wise ones listened for God in dreams as they considered what they needed to do and where they needed to go. Modern human beings consumed with outer reality have a tendency to leave dreaming behind. That is truly a loss. The dream bears important messages from the unconscious, which is always in communication with the inner community. This

---

4. The writings of Morton Kelsey, Bob Haden, and Jack Sanford are especially helpful for understanding dreams and the life of faith. For further reading please consult Kelsey, *Dreams: A Way to Listen to God* (Paramus, NJ: Paulist Press, 1978); Kelsey, *God, Dreams, and Revelation: A Christian Interpretation of Dreams*, revised and expanded edition (Minneapolis, MN: Augsburg Press, 1991); Sanford, *Dreams: God's Forgotten Language* (1968; San Francisco: HarperCollins, 1989); Haden, *Unopened Letters from God: Using Biblical Dreams to Unlock Nightly Dreams* (Asheville, NC: Haden Institute Publishing, 2010).

wisdom may prove critical to the overall process of self-discovery and ultimate wellness.

Listening for the Still, Small Voice

While we don't know much about Jesus and his dream life, we know he sought time away from the crowd and was deeply aware of what God meant for him to do. Yes, he was God, but he was also human, *and* he promised that we would do greater work than he did. So, there must be a way for the followers of Jesus today to find our own deep connections to the divine. We can come to understand the inner community that lives in our hearts and minds, so that we are more free to listen to the same still, small voice of God that spoke to the prophet Elisha after the earthquake, distinct from all the other loud voices that did not contain the voice of God.

It is the still, small voice of God that provides the information about when, how, and to what one must turn. Our inner work is about creating the inner space that allows us to hear that voice. We must constantly seek to find enough silence inside us and our worlds that we can hear the voice of God.

I find that observing silence and journaling are also more appropriate spaces for doing head and heart work than in the public arena of the larger community. Many of our inner community issues get brought to the larger outer community and end up being divisive and counterproductive. Perhaps one of the greatest causes of strife in our churches and other communities rises from a lack of discernment about what is an inner community issue versus an outer community issue.

Is this an issue between me and another person, to be addressed out in public? Maybe, or perhaps it is work best addressed within the inner community. If we're seeking to make a real turn and embrace lasting healing, the shadow energy needs to be named, confronted, and transformed in whatever ways are necessary. Then the turn is rooted in a new way of seeing. *Then* there is true healing, and the person making the projections becomes stronger and becomes better able to recognize the negative energy and reaction the next time it comes forward.

Merging Head and Heart, Inner and Outer

While this lengthy discussion might seem to be all about knowledge and the work of the intellect or the head, it is not. It is about both the head and the heart. Knowledge is critical as we live our lives with strength, power, and integrity, but the heart has to inform the knowledge as well.

The Spirit also plays a crucial role, as we recognize more and more that everything is not up to us and what we think. On our best days, when we are willing to tell ourselves the truth, we can confess our dependence upon God and our total inability to do anything good without God's amazing grace.

Unfortunately, our Western mentality and great capacity for achievement together hinder our ability to depend on the grace of God every minute of every day. We have a grave sense of misplaced power. We confuse our ability to be creative and inventive and effective with actually being in control. Painful as it is to admit, we cannot control our ego and we have little knowledge about how everything really works in this vast universe. This conflict makes it even more challenging to turn ourselves around. As I said at the start, repentance on a daily basis really is a tough assignment for all of us.

What, then, does it take? Faith, hope, and an outer community that can be trusted all help us to turn in new and better directions. I cannot overstate the necessity to walk with others each day on the pilgrim journey. While I have said much about the importance of inner community work, turning is ultimately not a solo enterprise. It is a great mistake to think that one can do all the inner reflection and opening to the work of the Spirit alone. The journey to a new way of seeing and being is engaged best when both the individual *and* the outer community work cooperatively.

We need one another in order to form the supportive relationships that help give us the courage to stay faithful to the work of turning when we know we have to make a turn. We provide for each other the necessary love, support, encouragement, affirmation of our worth, and many other gifts that are often difficult to name. This helps us to maintain the process of self-interrogation, allowing the release of inner community members that need to be set free and the death of ones that insist on being a source of negative energy.

In many ways this process is a bit like unraveling a large ball of thread. We can do it because it is on a spool that we can rewind at any point. The trusted community is much like the spool; it assists us in resetting and rewinding ourselves as necessary along the way. For me, this happens especially when we gather around the table for the Holy Meal week after week. We reaffirm that we can make the journey to new life, because we are not in the struggle alone. No matter how complex the inner community work might be, we can hold on because we have advocates and companions.

The only way to fully live the Way of Love is by letting go of all of the ways we project, invent, and create ourselves and others, and instead turn ourselves over to the God whose love is perfect. This is the good news: that God is always on the journey with the pilgrims and all of the questions, doubts, fears, and many selves that live in us, so we can find refuge in that amazing love that never leaves us. We can turn at any moment and God will be present to receive us, because God is present, always.

CHAPTER 3

Learn: Finding Meaning in God's Story

Dwight Zscheile

LEARN: Reflect on Scripture each day, especially on Jesus's life and teachings

"Those who love me will keep my word, and my Father will love them, and we will come to them and make our home with them."

—John 14:23

By reading and reflecting on Scripture, especially the life and teachings of Jesus, we draw near to God and God's word dwells in us. When we open our minds and hearts to Scripture, we learn to see God's story and God's activity in everyday life.[1]

---

1. "Learn," Episcopal Church, https://episcopalchurch.org/way-of-love/practice/learn.

I didn't grow up in the church. Even though I had been baptized as an infant, our family didn't go to church, and the stories and practices of Christianity didn't function in my household. I became a Christian as a young adult primarily through two influences: a friend who modeled Jesus's Way for me, calling into question my values and assumptions; and encountering a story from Scripture in two books I was assigned in a high school English class. These books (by Dickens and Dostoevsky) have characters who must make a big life choice at a turning point.

That story was from John's Gospel, where Jesus raises his friend Lazarus from the dead (John 11:1–44). It wasn't even the whole story that caught my attention; it was Jesus's conversation with Lazarus's sister Martha:

> Martha said to Jesus, "Lord, if you had been here, my brother would not have died. But even now I know that God will give you whatever you ask of him." Jesus said to her, "Your brother will rise again." Martha said to him, "I know that he will rise again in the resurrection on the last day." Jesus said to her, "I am the resurrection and the life. Those who believe in me, even though they die, will live, and everyone who lives and believes in me will never die. Do you believe this?" (John 11:21–26)

To my surprise, I felt myself answering *Yes, I believe this*. Now, I didn't really know what that meant. I wasn't yet connected to a church or faith community. There wasn't anyone in my life I could turn to who could explain the gospel to me. But there was a sense of ultimate hope and possibility in Jesus's words unlike anything I had ever heard. I knew that I needed to learn more about this story.

The Stories That Shape Our Lives

We all live our lives within stories. To be human is to interpret our experience through a repertoire of meanings. This repertoire comes from our families of origin, our communities, our friends, our cultures, our society—a whole variety of sources. Our experience shapes this repertoire in turn. We learn whether the world is trustworthy or untrustworthy, full of love, hate, or a mix of both. We are narrative creatures. To be human is to make meaning. When we fail to do so, we become depressed and fall into despair.

There are many sources of meaning in today's world, many stories that shape people's ways of seeing and inhabiting the world. For me, growing up in a secular home on the California coast, I was formed in a story that said life was a quest of individual self-discovery and striving. I assumed that I had to prove my worth, to justify myself, and to work hard to improve the world. It was all up to me. If I made a mistake, there wasn't much room for forgiveness. It was easy to be judgmental. In this story, everyone is supposed to make it up as she or he goes along. Established traditions and structures for human life are held lightly and easily jettisoned.

Even by the end of high school, this story was increasingly hollow to me. There was no basis for enduring community, no means of mutual recognition and reconciliation across social and cultural differences, and little ground for hope. I felt caught. I was yearning for a better, more adequate story, though I couldn't name it at the time. That is when the gospel surprised me. It surprised me with the story of Jesus, who embodied a more profound love than I had ever imagined.

In today's culture, to talk about "the good life" seems quaint. Many people are more concerned with simply surviving the torrent of busyness, disruption, and chaos brought by technological acceleration and social, cultural, and economic change. Over the generations, philosophers have long tried to articulate what constitutes a good life—a human life well lived. When I met Jesus, I discovered the answer to that question. Here was the touchstone for what humanity looked like in its fullness—a life in loving relationship or communion with God and others. To follow Jesus was to learn and begin to live his story.

The Bible in the Church Today

The Episcopal Church and other mainline Protestant denominations today have a complicated relationship with the Bible. On the one hand, it is foundational for the church's life and worship (much of the Book of Common Prayer is composed of Scripture, for instance). On the other hand, it tends to underfunction in the lives of many members. I remember a moment years ago in the congregation I serve where a member approached me at coffee hour and said, "I used to be Baptist, and I always felt guilty about not reading the Bible. But when I became Episcopalian I stopped feeling guilty about not reading it." Somehow, she had picked up the message in the Episcopal Church that reading the Bible was optional or unimportant. Another lifelong Episcopalian quietly told me once that she never really learned much about the Bible in confirmation and didn't really know how to access it or what to do with it. I suspect these sentiments are not rare.

Part of the reason for this is that the Bible is indeed a hard book—hard to make sense of across vast cultural differences from contemporary society; hard to understand in its nuance, complexity, and apparent contradictions; and hard to know what to make of texts that seem harsh, violent, or exclusive. Many of us have seen the Bible used as a weapon in the culture wars; some of us have been wounded. Some have experienced the Bible as a source of judgment and shame more than of grace and healing.

For these reasons, it can seem easier to minimize or explain away the Bible rather than to enter it courageously, curiously, and wholeheartedly. Understanding the cultural and historical conditions of the biblical writings is critically important to a deeper understanding, as is engaging the long tradition of commentary in the Jewish and Christian communities about biblical texts. Like Jacob wrestling with the angel in Genesis 32, the church has had—and should have!—a long and passionate relationship with the Bible. Jacob is renamed through his encounter (to Israel, "one who wrestles with God"). The church too finds its identity in wrestling with the stories of the Bible, especially the stories and words of Jesus.

Unfortunately, the Bible's difficulty has led some churches at times to err on the side of treating the Bible like an object to be taken apart, deconstructed, and dismissed. Challenging passages are simply explained away, rather than wrestled with faithfully. Expert leaders and teachers (typically clergy) reserve for themselves the power to interpret the Bible for the people, rather than finding ways to open up the Bible's richness and complexity for the people to interpret together in a participatory manner. Let me be clear: expertise in reading the Bible is immensely valuable for the reasons identified above. At the same time, clericalism and reliance on academic expertise can distance people from the Bible rather than help them enter into it.

As such, the core Christian spiritual practice of "Learn" can default into a merely academic and intellectual exercise conducted by church professionals rather than a means by which all of God's people come to make deeper and more faithful Christian meaning of their lives. For the Episcopal Church and other denominations that value education and tend to attract well-educated members, this is a ready temptation. When the church hasn't always helped its ordinary disciples to access and make sense of the Bible, they are often more than willing to steer clear of it or leave it in the hands of professional experts. This is perfectly understandable when such members feel incompetent and worry that they will have the wrong answer. The people end up disempowered, and the kind of learning of Scripture that is essential for discipleship ends up being short-circuited.

Making Meaning in a Secular Age

In contemporary Western culture, there is a more basic current at play that makes forming Christian identity and meaning difficult.

We live in what the philosopher Charles Taylor calls a "secular age," where it is assumed one can lead a perfectly good life without God.[2] In a secular age, human life is restricted to the immanent frame—concrete material existence, without reference to any transcendent power or presence. Humanity is understood to be on its own to make its own way, find its own purpose, and create a good society. There are no transcendent sources of authority to whom we are accountable, only the rules we make up ourselves. Daily life plays out in this restricted worldview.

Life in the secular age would seem very strange to most human societies in history and in the world today, where the numinous realm of God, the gods, spirits, or ancestors is more real than the everyday material world. For them, that world is charged with spiritual presence and power that one must reckon with. This is the world of the Bible, the world in which Jesus performed miraculous healings, cast out demons, and raised Lazarus from the dead. Many cultures in the world today read those biblical stories and can resonate viscerally with the cosmos they describe because it is not too far from their own.

In a secular age, it is very difficult for people to imagine and be led by the power and presence of God. The culture conspires against it, suggesting that we are on our own, that technology and human ingenuity alone will save us, that the only sources of meaning and identity are located inside our individual selves, that we are

---

2. See Charles Taylor, *A Secular Age* (Cambridge, MA: Harvard University Press, 2007).

not accountable to anyone or anything beyond ourselves. For this reason, God recedes into the background, perhaps as a moral anchor we hope is there because we fear without it there is only chaos, or as a feeling we sometimes get that comes and goes.

Yet even in contemporary Western culture, echoes of transcendence remain. Most of us are haunted by the spiritual and yearn on some level for its depths amidst the flatness of life in a secular age. Many people have experiences of being caught up short, of inexplicable connection with another person or place, of fullness, serenity, or mystery that the secular age can't explain. It's no wonder vampires, Harry Potter, and the like are so popular, evoking a magical world that many people in the modern West can't quite let go of.

Reading the Bible in a secular age means taking a trip into a different cosmos, a cosmos charged with divine agency and presence. Being Christian means trusting that this reality is actually ultimate— that the universe is created and sustained by a divine community of love (the Trinity) whose life is open and self-giving. Christianity is not just a set of moral prescriptions, either for individual holiness or creating a righteous and just society. It is a whole way of seeing and inhabiting the world that calls into question the assumptions of a secular age. Following Jesus means orienting one's life around his vision and teachings, which we come to embody ourselves (albeit imperfectly) through practicing his Way. It means participating through the power of the Holy Spirit in the divine life, both in the ordinary, mundane, here and now, and eternally.

Learning to Make Christian Meaning

The practice of learning God's story through the Bible is essential so that we can take this journey and live in this promise. Where a secular age narrows our sources of meaning, purpose, and identity only to what we can grasp with our senses, the Bible invites us to live fully in the world while being grounded in the life and love of God, which frees us from guilt, shame, and the fear of death. As Paul says so powerfully in Romans 8:

> There is therefore now no condemnation for those who are in Christ Jesus. . . . For I am convinced that neither death, nor life, nor angels, nor rulers, nor things present, nor things to come, nor powers, nor height, nor depth, nor anything else in all creation, will be able to separate us from the love of God in Christ Jesus our Lord. (Rom. 8:1, 38–39)

This is the promise we receive in Christ: we are joined to God and all others who share in this promise in a love that prevails over whatever life can throw at us. We have an identity and destiny as precious children of God that we can neither earn nor lose.

So how do we learn to live in that identity day to day? In many congregations, the predominant spirituality is a performative one—church professionals (clergy, staff, paid musicians, etc.) perform the faith for the people. Clergy are expected to read and interpret the Bible, pray, evangelize, and otherwise perform discipleship and ministry on behalf of the people. However, Christianity is not a spectator sport, and we live in a participatory age. We need to cultivate a more deeply *participatory* spirituality, rather than primarily a performative one. That means helping every member of the church read and interpret the Bible, pray, evangelize, and share in discipleship and ministry in their daily lives and spheres of influence.

Immersing ourselves in the story of God and God's people in Scripture, especially the stories and teachings of Jesus, is essential to this. When these stories become habitual, when they get in our bloodstream, when they function like a pair of lenses we wear through the day, then our imagination and behavior change too. We see people not "from a human point of view" (2 Cor. 5:16), but as the beloved people they are in God's eyes. We see hope and possibility where there was only despair and loss, amidst the crucified and forsaken places in our world. We resist the temptation to vengeance and bitterness and are able to extend forgiveness and peace, because God has forgiven us.

In October 2006, a gunman stormed into an Amish schoolhouse in rural Pennsylvania, taking ten girls hostage. He eventually shot eight of them (five of whom died) before taking his own life. The local Amish community, who were suffering the unimaginable loss of these children, reached out to the perpetrator's family and offered comfort, forgiveness, and even financial assistance. The secular media were astounded at these actions. For the Amish, it made perfect sense, for they had been praying the Lord's Prayer every day ("Forgive us our sins, as we forgive those who sin against us"). Their minds, hearts, and habits had been shaped at a deep level by Jesus's story.

Practices of Learning God's Story

Christians have cultivated many ways to learn God's story over the centuries. In this chapter, I will highlight a small number that I have found particularly meaningful in my work with congregations over the years and in my own life. Spiritual practices are a matter of discernment for each of us, both in our personalities and in varying seasons of our lives. There were things I needed as a new Christian that I find less helpful now. It is normal to try on and test out various forms of learning God's story over the course of our journey of faith. While the core practices of the Way of Love are essential, no one size fits all in how we express them at a particular moment.

Lectio Divina

The practice of *lectio divina* (literally "divine reading") has roots in the first centuries of Christianity and was developed in the late classical and early medieval periods. It is a way of engaging a biblical text by reading, meditating, praying, and contemplating God revealed in it. The point is not so much abstracting a theological principle or life lesson from the text as it is letting the text soak in, ruminating on it, and seeking spiritual illumination through it.

The assumption in *lectio divina* is that God will speak to us through the text, that the text is a way into closer communion with God. Thus, the practice combines careful and attentive reading with a posture of prayer, openness, and meditation. In *lectio divina*, we listen to the text as a way to listen to God's voice in our lives. *Lectio divina* can be done individually or in community.

Gospel-Based Discipleship

This practice of listening to Scripture in community was developed by indigenous Anglicans in North America and other parts of the world. It invites participants to encounter the gospel through three primary questions that are asked about a text as it is read three times: *What words or ideas did you hear? What is Jesus (the gospel) saying to you? What is Jesus (the gospel) calling you to do?* The spirit of Gospel-Based Discipleship, like *lectio divina*, is one of wonder, curiosity, and connection—to God, to the biblical story, to our own stories and lives, and to each other's stories. Sometimes a different translation is used in each reading of the text so that people can hear it afresh each time.

In Gospel-Based Discipleship, anyone can lead the session. No experts are required. Everyone has a place in the circle of listening and discernment. It is not about having the right or wrong answer about a text, but rather entering into the text and each other's stories imaginatively. The final question includes an invitation to action. This practice helps connect God's story to our own daily walk of discipleship.[3]

Dwelling in the Word

Dwelling in the Word is a contemporary practice derived from the tradition of *lectio divina*. Like Gospel-Based Discipleship, it is designed to deepen our ability to listen to God and each other

---

3. See *A Disciple's Prayer Book*, https://www.episcopalchurch.org/library/document/disciples-prayer-book.

through listening to the Bible together in community. First, choose a biblical passage, which can vary from a few verses to a good portion of a chapter. As the text is read out loud, people are invited to listen to what catches their imagination, what they have a question about in the text, or what the Spirit might be saying to them personally or to the group through the text.

After the text is read, there is a minute of silent reflection. Then people are invited to pair with a "reasonably friendly looking stranger"—someone they don't know particularly well. In pairs, each person takes turns sharing what she or he heard or wondered about in the text. This is a time of deep listening, because when the pairs return to the larger group, people are invited to share with the larger group (or table) a summary of what they heard their *partner* say, not what they said about the text. This can be difficult! Listening closely enough to another person that we can give public voice (literally "advocate") for them is a rare practice in today's society.

Dwelling in the Word is a transformational practice for congregations to adopt when they are seeking to grow in their capacity to discern God's leading. I have done it with groups as small as a handful of people and with rooms full of hundreds. Dwelling invites everyone to have a say and to be heard. It allows for the possibility of a multitude of interpretations, insights, and questions to be surfaced. In churches that can tend toward clericalism, dwelling can be an empowering practice since it is so deeply participatory.[4] It can also

---

4. For more details on Dwelling in the Word, see http://www.church innovations.org/2015/09/01/dwelling-in-the-word/.

be deeply indicative, to groups large and small, of where the Spirit is leading the church, an instrument of discernment.

Bible Study

The first three practices listed above are focused on spiritual listening, either alone or in community. They do not stress deep intellectual, critical, or historical engagement with a biblical text. Bible study is a vital and complementary way to learn God's story by doing so. There are many ways to do Bible study either individually or in a group. It typically involves some analytical tools, historical background, or other teaching material that fleshes out the context of a biblical passage. It brings in expertise from scholars or facilitators who can illuminate dimensions of the Bible that might otherwise be obscure. This kind of engagement enriches and opens up biblical texts, particularly across the cultural gulf between the setting of their origin and today. Bible study that goes deep into a book of the Bible or explores a theme or section over time is an essential part of learning God's story.

Scripture Memorization

This practice tends to be rare in mainline Protestant communities, but it is worth claiming. When we choose a brief passage of the Bible and commit it to heart, those words come alive in us and enter our thoughts and imagination like the words of a favorite song. We find them appearing when we need them, in times of adversity and joy. Psalm 23 is a favorite for many people, but there are countless other texts that are fruitful for memorization. Choose a few as you read through the Bible that speak particularly powerfully to you. The ancient monastic fathers and mothers of the desert used memorization of Scripture as a way to cultivate an awareness of the Divine presence—in themselves and in everyone they met.

Spiritual Storytelling

It is vital to practice making spiritual meaning of our own experience by sharing spiritual stories. We don't practice this often enough in most congregations.

Perhaps the simplest place to begin is by gathering people and inviting them to pair and share a story of a time when they felt most spiritually alive or energized, taking turns sharing about five to eight minutes each. I have done this with many groups over the years and every single time the buzz in the room has been palpable. Everyone has a story to share. It is important that the prompt be simple and accessible. People can go as deep as they feel comfortable with.

My colleague Michael Binder did this once with a group in a congregation and at a break, four women came up to him, a few in tears. They had been friends for four decades together in the same church, but this was the first time they had shared these spiritual stories with each other. Another colleague, Andrew Root, interviewed members of several congregations to hear some of their most powerful stories of encountering God. They articulated moving stories of divine action in their lives, but also told him they had never been asked to share these stories at church or with their pastors. [5]

In order for people in congregations to make Christian spiritual meaning of their lives and world, the church must help them both enter and engage the biblical story and practice telling their own stories. When we do these in conjunction together over time, the stories come to intersect more and more deeply. We begin to find the touchpoints between God's story in the Bible and our own experience. We begin to name what is at stake in both the biblical stories and in our own stories. New meaning surfaces, and with that meaning, hope.

Christian leadership is primarily about helping people make spiritual meaning of their lives.[6] It involves cultivating the spaces, practices, and habits where people learn to understand themselves as part of God's great story. This story is still playing out in the world today. It encompasses faithful ancestors from across the world and across the ages. It comes to life in the local and ordinary, which is where Jesus joins us in the incarnation.

---

5. See Andrew Root, *Christopraxis: A Practical Theology of the Cross* (Minneapolis: Fortress Press, 2014).
6. See Scott Cormode, *Making Spiritual Sense* (Nashville: Abingdon Press, 2006).

Learning God's story is not only an exercise of the head, but something we practice with our whole selves through actions like biblical interpretation and storytelling in community. In a moment in our society and world where there are innumerable stories that are distorted, meaningless, and ultimately lead to despair, learning and living God's story can raise us, like Lazarus, to new life.

CHAPTER 4

Pray

David Vryhof

PRAY: Dwell intentionally with God each day

He was praying in a certain place, and after he had finished, one of his disciples said to him, "Lord, teach us to pray, as John taught his disciples."

—Luke 11:1

Jesus teaches us to come before God with humble hearts, boldly offering our thanksgivings and concerns to God or simply listening for God's voice in our lives and in the world. Whether in thought, word or deed, individually or corporately, when we pray we invite and dwell in God's loving presence.[1]

Prayer is a gift to be received, not a task to be completed. As a monastic, I know this to be true.

---

1. "Pray," Episcopal Church, https://episcopalchurch.org/way-of-love/practice/pray.

When we approach prayer as a task, it quickly becomes a burden. We feel guilty that we are "not praying enough" (how much would "enough" be, actually?); we chide ourselves for our lack of self-discipline, and we envy those who seem to have a deep and consistent "prayer life." If you recognize yourself in this description, you are not alone. Perhaps you've asked yourself, "Why do I so consistently find myself failing in prayer even though I believe in its importance?"

Something changes when we begin to think of prayer as a gift rather than as a task. A gift is freely given by another; we have only to receive it. In prayer, God offers us not only God's own self, but also *everything we need* to live abundant and fruitful lives: gifts of love, forgiveness, wisdom, guidance, strength, and more. Our part is simply to open our hearts to receive these gifts.

Christians believe that *God* is the giver of all good things, and that God is and always has been the *initiator*, throughout the whole of salvation history. It is *God* who created the world and all that it contains; we owe our very existence to God's initiative. It was *God* who established a covenant with Abraham, *God* who delivered the Israelites from bondage in Egypt and provided for them in the wilderness, *God* who gave the Law to Moses and led the people to the Promised Land. It was *God* who rescued them from exile in Babylon and brought them home, and *God* who sent prophets to guide them and kings to lead them.

Despite their stubbornness and resistance, God continued to reach out to them, time and time again, rescuing them from their folly, forgiving them, and restoring them to communion with God's self. Finally, when the appointed time had come, it was *God* who so loved the world that he sent his only begotten Son, that all might have new and eternal life in him.

We affirm that God is the initiator, always reaching out to us in love. Prayer, too, is initiated by God. It is God who stirs our hearts to seek him; God who enkindles our passion and desire to love and be loved by him. *God* is the initiator of every form of prayer. Consider these examples:

- Our hearts are stirred by the sight of a brilliant sunset and we are moved to offer a prayer of *thanks and praise.*
- We are touched by the suffering of others and inspired to make *intercession* for them.
- Our hearts are awakened to the ways in which we have failed to love God and our neighbors, and a prayer of *contrition or confession* rises from our hearts.
- We are inspired to offer our money and time, even our very selves, to God, but it is the Spirit who has inspired this prayer of *oblation and self-offering* in us.

Always it is God's Spirit at work in us, helping us to notice, moving us to care, guiding our consciousness, leading us in love. Our prayers are a response to the Spirit's activity in our hearts.

The Posture of Receptivity

If God is the initiator of every form of prayer, then the primary *posture* of prayer is a posture of receptivity, of attentiveness, of listening and watching, of receiving. God is revealing God's self to us in every moment of every day—in the beauty of creation that surrounds us ("The heavens declare the glory of God and the firmament shows forth his handiwork" [Ps. 19:1]), in our human interactions, in the words of others that we read or hear, in times of worship and in times of silent solitude, in music and art and dance. Grace is everywhere; we have only to notice and receive it.

The apostle Paul tells us to "pray without ceasing" (1 Thess. 5:17). We cannot, of course, remain in our prayer corner all day and all night. But could we learn to remain in this posture of receptivity throughout the day, as we interact with others and carry out our tasks? Could we learn to pay attention to the movements of grace—in the world around us, in our daily interactions, and in ourselves? Could we listen for God's voice and watch for God's activity as we move through our days? Could we be attentive, receptive, watchful—and in this way, "pray without ceasing"?

A simple but wise woman once remarked, "I think finding God is similar to what happens when I play 'hide and seek' with the little ones. When I hide, I always leave a little of myself 'sticking out.' If I hide behind the curtain, I let my shoes stick out; if I'm behind a tree, I let my sleeve show—because I want them to find me." Though we cannot see God or hear God or touch God in the same ways that we are able to see or hear or touch one another, God still "sticks out" in a thousand ways each day, if we have eyes and ears that are open, that watch and listen for God's presence and activity. God "sticks out" because God wants to be found by us. To learn to pray without ceasing in this way—watching and listening for God in every moment of every day—is to learn not only to pray, but to pray our lives.

Rather than waking up in the morning and saying to ourselves, "Where am I going to find the time to pray today, when there are so many other things to be done?" we say, "How will God 'stick out' for me today? Where will I see God's grace at work? How will I hear God's voice today? How will God be communicating with me, inviting me into a more intimate communion with God's self, in this sacred and special day? Where, and how, will I discover God's love present and active today?" The first question in this list views prayer as a *task*; the others view prayer as a *gift* God wants to give us, which may come to us at any moment.

In prayer, we are meant to receive God's precious gifts, which we so need. And yet so many of us lack a sense of anticipation, of expectancy, as we begin our day. We are surprised when God shows up. What might we notice if we began our day convinced that God was going to be in it?

I once met with a group of Christians and asked them how many years they had served God in their various ministries. The answers came: eighteen years, seven years, twenty-three years, and so on. (There was a good deal of ministerial experience in that room.) "And how many of you have heard God expressing deep appreciation and gratitude for all you have done?" I asked. They were silent. Some exchanged puzzled glances. "What kind of God is it that you serve," I asked, "who never acknowledges or expresses appreciation for all you have sacrificed, for all you continue to sacrifice, to make yourselves available for God and God's people? I am thoroughly

convinced that God's heart is overflowing with gratitude for the generosity and diligence and love you have offered in the service of the
gospel. I believe God wants each of you to know that your sacrifices
and your tireless efforts are seen and valued."

It is in prayer that we can receive this love, affirmation, and gratitude; in prayer we discover that we are seen and valued, appreciated,
and loved. "We love because [God] first loved us," writes the author
of 1 John (4:19). Prayer is the place where we receive this love, where
we find consolation and healing and power and courage to be God's
people in the world.

"We love because God first loved us." In prayer we come to
know ourselves as beloved children of God. This is who we are, our
primary identity and claim. This identity—beloved child of God—
is far more important than any identity based on talent or wealth
or achievement or social status. It changes us. Having discovered
the freedom and joy of this identity ourselves, we can then share it
with others. Having received God's love, we can offer that same love
to others. Having known God's forgiveness ourselves, we can learn
to forgive others. When we realize that we ourselves have not been
judged by God, we can withhold our judgment of others. We love
in the same ways we have been loved, and this is the work of prayer:
to receive the great gift of God's love, to notice how it surrounds us
each day, to take in the gift and allow it to transform us.

Imagine this: a group of small children are playing in a sandbox
in the park while their parents watch them from a nearby bench.
Suddenly a boy pops up, walks over to his mother, and leans against
her. She gives him a hug, rubs his back, and kisses his forehead. After

a minute or two, he returns to play. He needed for a moment to be in her presence, to feel her love, to be assured that he was safe. Prayer is something like that—a pause in the busyness of our day in which we withdraw to rest a while and to receive God's assurance that we are beloved children of God. That is why we set apart time to pray; that is why we go on retreat. We need this connection to Love in order to thrive.

Abiding in Prayer

All of this we see in the life of Jesus, who is "the image of the invisible God" (Col. 1:15). At the beginning of his ministry, Jesus receives a powerful affirmation at the moment of his baptism that he is God's beloved Son, in whom God is well pleased (Luke 3:21–22). From that point on, he dwells in this knowledge and in this intimate relationship with the One he calls his "Father," at every moment relying completely on this bond of love for all that he needs. All of his words and all of his actions flow from the deep union he shares with the Father, in whom he constantly abides. "Very truly, I tell you," he says to his followers, "the Son can do nothing on his own, but only what he sees the Father doing; for whatever the Father does, the Son does likewise" (John 5:19).

Moment by moment, Jesus "abides" in the Father, deeply connected to God, seeking not his own will but the will of the Father. His life is an ongoing prayer. He is guided and held, day by day, in this intimate union, and he says this can be our experience as well. "Abide in me as I abide in you," he says, "Just as the branch cannot bear fruit by itself unless it abides in the vine, neither can you unless you abide in me" (John 15:4).

Jesus lived constantly in communion and in communication with God. What will help us to live prayerfully, in a posture of openness and receptivity, listening and watching to discern the desire of God in every situation? What will help us "abide" in Christ?

In *The Way of a Pilgrim,* a village priest gives some very authoritative advice on prayer: "If you want to be pure, right, and enjoyable, you must choose some short prayer, consisting of few but forcible words, and repeat it frequently, over a long period. Then you will find delight in prayer."[2] A simple phrase, lovingly repeated, that turns our hearts toward God is all that is needed.

The same idea is found in the practice of Brother Lawrence, a seventeenth-century lay brother in a Carmelite monastery in Paris. In his letters, he writes:

> I do not advise you to use multiplicity of words in prayer; many words and long discourses being often the occasions of wandering. . . . One way to recollect the mind easily in the time of prayer, and preserve it more in tranquility, is not to let it wander too far at other times; you should keep it strictly in the presence of God; and being accustomed to think of him often, you will find it easy to keep your mind

---

2. Simon Tugwell, OP, *Prayer: Living with God* (Springfield, IL: Templegate, 1975), 61.

calm at the time of prayer, or at least to recall it from its wanderings.[3]

There are many ways to grow in our capacity to practice the attentiveness and receptivity that will help us recognize and receive God's gifts of love. Silence helps. In silence, we still the clamor of our inner lives. We allow God's peace to descend on us, to calm and quiet us, so that we may "be still and know" that God is God (Ps. 46:10). A jar containing water and sand will be cloudy when shaken, but will settle and become clear when left to be still. So our busy inner worlds can be quieted so that we can see clearly what we ought to see, and rightly judge what we ought to do. In silence, we learn to listen to the voice of the Shepherd ("My sheep hear my voice. I know them, and they follow me," John 10:27). We grow in our ability to discern that voice from all the voices that assault us daily, from within and without.

There are voices that live within us: the voice of courage and the voice of shame, the voice of self-interest and the voice of compassion, the voice of resentment and the voice of generosity. There are also voices that come from outside of us: the voices of our parents, our teachers, our friends, our heroes, as well as the voices of advertising, of our consumerist culture, of those whose values stand in opposition to the ways of God. We have little hope of distinguishing

---

3. Br. Lawrence of the Resurrection (1614–1691), in *Letters of Brother Lawrence*, quoted in: Tugwell, *Prayer: Living with God*, 61.

between these voices, and recognizing the voice of the Savior, if we cannot be still long enough to learn to listen.

When I was young, a music teacher taught us the sounds of various instruments of the orchestra. "This is the sound of a flute," she would say, "and this is the melody line that the flute plays. Listen carefully to it and try to remember it." Then she would put on the recording of the whole orchestra and ask us to concentrate and to raise our hands when we heard the sound of the flute or recognized its melody. We were being trained to distinguish the "voice" of the flute amidst all the other "voices" that made up the orchestra. This, too, is the work of prayer: to be still, to listen attentively, to come to know the voice of the Good Shepherd, so that we can pick it out even when it is surrounded by so many other voices and sounds. "My sheep hear my voice."

Giving God Our Full Attention

"I pray as I drive to work," one person says. "It is the only time when I can be alone to pray." "This is a good thing," I answer, "I am glad that you can be aware of God's presence with you as you drive to work each day, and I hope that you can extend that mindfulness throughout your day, so that you are aware of God surrounding you in love no matter what you might be doing. But still, is there any time when God gets your *full* attention?"

In the intimacy of human relationships, we know the importance of giving the other our full attention. A husband who says to his wife, "Keep talking; I'm listening" while he continues to study his computer screen, will soon discover that this will not do. Spouses and partners and close friends need to find times when they can give one another their full attention. Intimacy requires it. So, too, in our relationship with God. If we hope to grow in love and deepen our intimacy, we simply must find time and space to give God our full attention.

Again, Jesus is our example. We see him regularly withdrawing from the company of others to go out into the wilderness, or up to the mountaintops, or into the stillness of a garden at night. He goes there to listen deeply, to quiet the tumult of his own heart, to receive all he needs in that moment from God. In these times he is able to give God his full attention, free from interruptions and distractions. We, too, need these times.

How might you weave these times of intimate communion with God into your own life? Could there be a time (or several times) each day when you pause in your activity to be still, to recall God's presence, to breathe, and to listen for God's voice? Is there a time (or times) each week or each month when you set aside a more substantial time to go deeper, to descend into stillness, to listen and watch and receive? What pattern might work best for you, given your life circumstances and your present responsibilities? Where might you find, or make, time for God?

Some people keep a simple Rule of Life, a set of guidelines which they have drafted to remind themselves of the practices that will keep them healthy and balanced, and focused on the things they value most. A Rule of Life is a specific (and realistic) plan for how we will prioritize and protect the sacred practices and habits that shape our lives. You might give thought to what rhythm of prayer and silence would best sustain you from day to day and week to week. Write down what you intend to do and try it out for several months.

Ways to Pray

Having set apart some times in which to give God our full attention, how shall we use the time? Is there a right way to pray? And which prayer methods are best?

There are many ways to pray, and there is no "right" way to pray that all should follow. Our experience of prayer will be as varied and interesting as our personalities and temperaments. Each person's relationship with God will be unique, and so each person's prayer will be unique. Resist the temptation to compare yourself or your practice to others; find your own way of being with God, the way that best suits your temperament and personality, and that feels most authentic to you.

Having said that, we also recognize the value of familiarizing ourselves with some of the ways to pray that have proven to be beneficial to many. Here are a few of them:

Discursive Prayer

A friendship deepens when two people share their thoughts and feelings with one another. So, too, in prayer we are invited into a relationship of love and intimacy in which we can freely share our thoughts and emotions with God. There are countless examples of this kind of discursive prayer in the psalms and throughout the Scriptures.

In the *Rule of Life of the Society of Saint John the Evangelist,* we say:

> (In prayer) we are called to offer all our work to God and ask for the graces we need to do it in Christ's name. In our prayer we are to test whether God is confirming our intentions and desires or not. We are able to pray about one another, our relationships and common endeavors. We are to bring him our sufferings and poverty, our passion and sexuality, our fears and resistances, our desires and dreams, our losses and grief. We must spread before him our cares about the world and its peoples, our friends and families, our enemies and those from whom we are estranged. Our successes and failures, our gifts and shortcomings are equally the stuff of prayer.[4]

There is nothing that is "off-limits" in prayer. If prayer is to be authentic, it must be honest; and for it to be honest, it must arise out of a relationship in which we know ourselves to be loved, unconditionally and forever. Only then can we disclose what is really going on in our lives and open ourselves to God's healing and guidance.

---

4. *Rule of the Society of Saint John the Evangelist* (Cambridge, MA: Cowley Publications, 1997), 45.

Meditative Prayer

"In our meditative prayer each of us seeks intimate communion with God. Quietness and freedom from interruption are needed for us to enter deeply into this prayer."[5] There are many ways in which we can practice this type of prayer, in which we "go deeper" in our relationship with God. The *SSJE Rule* goes on to say, "The focus of our meditation may be on the Word of God in Scripture or holy writings. We may use our imaginations to enter into the deep meaning of a scriptural story.[6] Or in slow, reflective reading[7] we may wait for the Spirit to alert us to the words or image which are to be the means of God's particular revelation to us on this day."[8]

Dominican theologian Simon Tugwell writes:

Somehow we must find a way of remembering God that does not work in fits and starts, but that will actually last through the day; a kind of fundamental remembrance of God that will affect our heart, and allow our most unpremeditated

---

5. Ibid, 46.

6. This prayer using the imagination is sometimes referred to as "Ignatian Meditation" because St. Ignatius employed it so frequently in his *Spiritual Exercises*. For an excellent description, see Martin L. Smith's *The Word Is Very Near You* (Cambridge, MA: Cowley Publications, 1989), chapter 7.

7. This prayer utilizing slow, reflective reading is sometimes referred to as *lectio divina* ("holy reading") or as "Benedictine Meditation" because of its prevalence in Benedictine monasteries. See Martin L. Smith's *The Word Is Very Near You,* chapter 8.

8. *Rule of the Society of Saint John the Evangelist,* 46.

and spontaneous behavior to be transformed, as it were, at the root. . . . Meditation can be seen as a kind of rehearsal for the unknown future; and the more diverse the material one has stored away in one's reserves, the better prepared one will be. . . . "Rehearse" is the basic meaning of the Latin word from which we get our word "meditation." . . . The basic meaning of "rehearse" is to rehearse one's lines.[9]

In meditative prayer, we come to know ourselves. We see not only our gifts and our strengths, but our places of weakness and vulnerability. We imagine the person we want to become and "rehearse" what we might say and do in different situations.

We may also employ icons, images, and symbols in our prayer. "Our prayer may distill our heart's desire in single words or hallowed phrases lovingly repeated, while we lay aside discursive thoughts in order to be unified with Christ. Or we may simply wait on God expectantly until our affections are kindled, and our hearts find a few words to give voice to our worship."[10]

In meditative prayer, then, we use words and images to draw us deeper into God's presence. We notice our thoughts and our feelings in response to a passage of Scripture, a picture, or an image, and we use these observations as springboards into deeper, more reflective prayer.

---

9. Tugwell, *Prayer: Living with God*, 4 6.
10. *Rule of the Society of Saint John the Evangelist*, 47.

65

Contemplative Prayer

Not everyone will be drawn to contemplation, the state of prayer in which we set aside thoughts and words and images and "surrender ourselves to the mystery beyond words of Christ's abiding in us, and our abiding in him close to the Father's heart."[11] In its purest sense, "contemplation" is the gift of God and not something we attain. Still there are ways of prayer, such as Centering Prayer, which prepare us to enter into the contemplative state by setting aside our thoughts in order to gaze with intention and loving desire on the mystery that is God, a mystery which is beyond all words and thoughts.

Praying in and with the natural world can be a great help to meditative or contemplative prayer. Listening, looking, and noticing open us to the wonder and gratitude that are at the heart of life. Prayer keeps wonder alive in us.

It is critical to remember that methods of prayer are a means to an end, not the end itself. We must free ourselves of the notion that there is a "right" way to pray or that there is a goal to be reached, lest we be so focused on the method or goal that we lose sight of the relationship prayer is meant to enhance.

Prayer as Relationship

Difficulties in prayer are to be expected. As in human relationships, there will be "dry patches" or seasons of strain or trouble that may

---

11. Ibid.

lead to a breakdown in communication or a feeling of estrangement from the other. It is not uncommon to go through similar experiences in our relationship with God. The intensity of feeling that characterized the early days of the relationship may eventually give way to a deeper union that does not depend on strong emotion to sustain it. The thing is to persevere, to keep "showing up," even when the initial excitement has worn off.

Difficult patches can, in fact, strengthen our human relationships as well as our relationship with God. And, as in human relationships, it's best to be honest and transparent, to uncover and name the obstacles that are keeping us from experiencing intimacy, and to work to solve these challenges. A spiritual director or a spiritual friend may be helpful to us in these times.

Some years ago I saw a movie in which two people met and fell in love. There was one particular scene in the movie that touched me deeply, when the lovers were lying in bed, facing each another, and speaking tenderly to one another as lovers do. It has become an icon for me of the deep and intimate relationship God longs for with each one of us.

This concept of prayer as a relationship between lovers is not new; there have been many expressions of it, especially in the Church's mystical tradition. The image is found in the Psalms, in the Song of Solomon, and in the writings of Christian mystics. It can be a helpful image, inviting us to a deeper relationship with God. Lovers long to know each other. They long to share their deepest desires and hopes and fears with the one they love because they know that these secrets will be accepted graciously and held respectfully. They can risk being vulnerable and open to one another.

A deep trust between the two people forms the foundation for intimate connection. They want to know and to be known, to love and to be loved. What is true in human relationships can also be true in our relationship with the Divine. Consider what it would feel like to speak with God or with Christ or with the Spirit as one would speak with a lover.

Lovers also share their passions and their vision. And shouldn't we come to know and love what God loves, to unite ourselves with God's purposes in the world? A loving relationship will weaken if the lovers are at cross purposes or cannot find shared values and priorities. So we might listen carefully for insights into God's ways, God's hopes, God's purposes in the world, being eager to cooperate with them and further their accomplishment.

Prayer will be expressed in a variety of ways in each of our lives. Some days, God will inspire us, like King David, to dance with joy before the Lord. Some days God will move us to lift our voices in song. Some days the Spirit may touch the place where we hurt; we may groan and lament. Some days God's invitation will be to quiet our hearts to listen deeply. Some days God will invite us to reflect (with God) on the world, on our neighbors, or on ourselves. There is no right way to pray. Pray in the way you are being invited to pray by the Spirit, and always pray as you can, not as you think you ought to pray.

Prayer is God's gift; you have only to open your heart to receive it.

CHAPTER 5

Worship

Frank Logue

WORSHIP: Gather in community weekly to thank, praise, and dwell with God

When he was at the table with them, he took bread, blessed and broke it, and gave it to them. Then their eyes were opened, and they recognized him.

—Luke 24:30–31

When we worship, we gather with others before God. We hear the Good News of Jesus Christ, give thanks, confess, and offer the brokenness of the world to God. As we break bread, our eyes are opened to the presence of Christ. By the power of the Holy Spirit, we are made one body, the body of Christ sent forth to live the Way of Love.[1]

---

1. "Worship," Episcopal Church, https://www.churchpublishing.org/way ofloveworship.

Worship offers each of us the opportunity to set aside time for an experience that reminds us there *is* a God and that God *is not us*. We acknowledge that God is worthy of our worship and praise, and we join our voices with others who do the same. This fourth practice takes us into the very heart of the Way of Love, because in worship we turn, learn, and pray as a gathered body and so are empowered to bless and go before we pause once more, finding our rest in God alone.

A Day and Time Set Apart

Our weekly worship on Sunday takes place out of time and on what the early church called the eighth day, the first day after the resurrection. Sunday was neither the Sabbath for Jews nor a day off in ancient Rome. The first Christians saw this day as breaking the constraints of the seven days. With eyes honed by apocalyptic literature to see the life of the world-to-come breaking into the here and now, they called it the eighth day. In our weekly worship we continue to acknowledge eternity has already begun and that something genuinely extra-ordinary is happening.

I experienced this truth recently, when I found myself standing on the street corner in Hawkinsville. The middle Georgia town of 4,600 souls was founded in 1830, and St. Luke's Episcopal Church was founded a few decades later. The people of Pulaski County know St. Luke's, but I still got some funny looks from passing cars as I waved while adorned in an ornate, green chasuble. The heavy poncho-like liturgical vestment was not optimal for the already hot summer morning, but it matched the altar frontal and was the norm for worship on the Sundays after Pentecost for the congregation. One of my fellow servers said with a twinkle in his eye, "You are freaking out the Baptists and Pentecostals."

Having spent a number of years of my childhood and teens in the Church of God, I knew he was right, but none of us minded. Those driving by were off to worship God in their way, and we were headed into St. Luke's to worship in our way.

I found myself drawn to liturgical worship for the ways it differs from daily life. In clothes that find their origins in the court vestments of the Roman Empire, and with servers gathered around an altar repeating long-prayed words, we share with fellow believers through the ages practices from another world. This might not have immediate appeal for everyone, but I have found it strangely effective for me. The strangeness is part of the gift of our worship. As Presiding Bishop Michael Curry said in a Way of Love Podcast on worship, "Where else do you take a glass of wine and some bread and make a fuss over it?"[2]

The fuss is not just the vestments, of course, but the vessels we use to show the Eucharist is a most special meal. In one church in our diocese, a set of silver dates back to Georgia's days as a colony. In another I see the name of the father of a friend from college etched into the base. At King of Peace (a church I planted after seminary), the vessels came from the pottery wheel of a fellow seminarian. In

---

2. Michael B. Curry, *The Way of Love*, podcast, season 1, episode 4, https.// wayoflove.episcopalchurch.org/episodes/season/1/episode/4.

every church where I worship, these are vessels set apart for sacred use in nourishing the people of God. From there, add on the lecterns with eagles, the pulpits with angels, the Gospel books covered in antique brass. Even in churches with less ornate furnishings, the sanctuary is clearly a place unlike those we encounter in the rest of our lives.

As the people of God gather in worship, we are reminded of the reality of the sacred all around us. Then we leave to be real estate agents, teachers, EMTs, plumbers, parents, and Scout leaders—and all to the glory of God. Every life in the world is already infused with the sacred. Worship—as a time set apart in a holy space with sacred vestments and vessels—reminds us of the divine in every part of our lives.

A Sacramental Worldview

When we worship in the Episcopal Church, as in other liturgical churches, sacraments are central to our gatherings. More than simply rituals performed by those who follow Jesus, sacraments train us to see the world as not separate from God but shot through with the presence of the divine. We see visible signs of the presence of an otherwise invisible God. In this way, Jesus himself was a living sacrament.

Sacraments are, in the words of the catechism found in our prayer book, "Outward and visible signs of an inward and spiritual grace."[3] They are the tangible ways we experience the unearned favor

---

3. The Episcopal Church, *The Book of Common Prayer* (New York: Church Publishing, 1979), 857 (hereafter BCP).

and love that are God's grace. For us, the two prime sacraments or vehicles for that grace are Baptism and Eucharist (the rites Jesus initiated in his earthly ministry).

Baptism is the ritual by which we renounce those things that pull us from God, ask forgiveness for our sins, and accept Jesus as our ruler and guide. You could call it the rite of turning. In the waters of baptism, we are united with Jesus in his death and made members of the body of Christ, the Church. Though some think of it as ritual bathing to wash us from sin, baptism is actually ritual drowning, as we die to ourselves and are born to new life. Water is the tangible sign of the grace of our adoption as redeemed children of God.

The Holy Eucharist is the central act of remembrance for Christians, yet in this moment the word "remember" has a deeper meaning. This is not "remember the time Jesus ate that last meal with his disciples." The Greek word here is *anamnesis*. To re-member is to assemble the members again. It can also be translated as to re-present, or to make present once again. The word conjures the notion of an arm that has been reattached after being cut off and dis-membered. This meaning matters most. Jesus is not just someone we recall. He becomes present to believers anew in the outward signs of bread and wine, and we are knit into his body like branches reattached to the vine.

There are five additional sacramental rites, which are means of grace: confirmation, when we make a mature commitment to our faith; ordination for those called to those roles within the body; marriage for persons entering a lifelong union; reconciliation of a penitent, which is a private confession with a priest who bestows pardon and absolution; and unction, which includes anointing the sick with oil and laying on of hands in prayer.

Beyond these rites, there are so many ways we see outward signs of God's grace and love. This is where poetry captures what often escapes doctrine. In her epic poem *Aurora Leigh*, Elizabeth Barrett Browning wrote,

> The whole temporal show related royally,
> And build up to eterne significance
> Through the open arms of God. . . .
> Earth's crammed with heaven,
> And every common bush afire with God;
> But only he who sees, takes off his shoes—
> The rest sit round it and pluck blackberries.

Everything we see as temporary and earthly has eternal significance because it has all been embraced in the arms of God. Earth itself is crammed full of heaven. Our worship of God in the sacraments of the church points us out into the world, where God's presence is waiting to be worshiped and acknowledged.

Dis-ease with the World

As different as the worship space is, our worship is designed to have a real impact on our daily lives and on the world far beyond the church. Faith in Jesus in its earliest days was something like an infectious disease. It was a disease if we understand this to mean a dis-ease with the world as it is. Those who came to see the world as Jesus saw it were no longer comfortable with the status quo. And it was infectious because the sense that the world was upside down and needed to be turned aright, *that* sense spread from person to person, rapidly taking over families and communities. In time parts of the whole Roman Empire were infected with the subversive good news that *all* are worthy of God's love, the last are first, and society's least important members—the widows and orphans—should be the concern of all.

It is easy to get inoculated with a less virulent strain of this dis-ease. One can catch a mild case of Christianity and so end up immune to a more virulent strain, as if by a vaccine. We can get a mild dose of "Jesus loves me this I know, for the Bible tells me so." We can worship when it is convenient and fit faith into a small Sunday box. We might end up feeling that I'm okay and you're okay and the world is more or less fine. But I am not okay. None of us is truly "okay." And our society is certainly not okay.

America is not in the midst of an opioid crisis by accident, but because of an overwhelming desire to numb the pain. We are surrounded by people wounded by people who were wounded by wounded people. We need healing. The pain can come from sexual, physical, and emotional abuse, sometimes caused by the Church itself. For many, the pain also comes from feeling like they will never measure up, or that they've disappointed God or themselves, or that they can't seem to stop acting in ways they know to be wrong. Jesus offers the antidote to the broken, destructive way of life most of us know too well. He calls us to repent and turn toward God, and gives us the grace and power to amend our lives. Where do we access that power to live subversive and Jesus-centered lives? Grounded in and nourished by word and sacrament in worship.

This can sound like stained-glass talk with no grounding in the real world, but I have watched a community live it out. When we started King of Peace Episcopal Church, the vision was to found a congregation that, if the doors closed a decade later, people who never attended would miss the church. We hoped to gather an assembly of the faithful who would bless and love the community around it.

Kingsland, Georgia, was composed mostly of families with young children, and 79 percent of the area was 39 or younger. Submarine Base Kings Bay was the major employer. In the founding decade, we baptized 118 people, which means we said these words from the baptismal liturgy again and again: "Will you who witness these vows do all in your power to support these persons in their life in Christ?" (BCP, 303). That promise had to extend beyond our own children, and into the community around us. In time, a disease with what our community lacked led to founding a full-day, full-year preschool for households where both parents worked. We started a Boy Scout troop and hosted Cub Scouts, a Venture Crew, and Girl Scouts.

When a parishioner was arrested for drug possession, we gained a new dis-ease. He needed to attend a weekly 12-step group, and none of the Alcoholics Anonymous groups wanted to welcome drug-addicted persons. Members of the congregation in recovery created a Narcotics Anonymous group that met twice a week. Soon it was filled with others struggling to drive to the next county north.

While the shape it takes will be different in every place, ending the liturgy "Go in peace to love and serve the Lord" (BCP, 340) is meant to lead to ways of serving that make that love of God real for those who would otherwise be left out. Worship is always tied closely to God's mission in the world. Worship is meant to equip and lead us to the practices of Bless and Go. It changes us and changes how we are in the world.

The Spiritual Practice of Worship

I remember when my young family decided we would shift from attending church whenever it was convenient to taking part in our home church's worship whenever we were in town and able to go. At the time, it didn't seem like a major decision, but that single commitment changed so much for us. It meant setting time apart to worship and dwell with God and with a specific community of people.

My wife, Victoria, and I had regularly worshipped together before our daughter, Griffin, was born, but we did so more sporadically than, well, religiously. We had promised at her baptism that she would be "brought up in the Christian faith and life" (BCP, 302). Still, by the time her third birthday approached and we had moved back to Rome, Georgia, it wasn't happening. As Lent approached, we decided to worship on Ash Wednesday and every Sunday leading up to Easter: a Lenten practice of regular worship. Once we had worshipped at noon on Wednesday, we enjoyed it enough to make that service a part of our Lenten practice as well.

By Holy Week, we had been regularly worshipping, and for all but the main Sunday Eucharist, it was mostly with the same smaller group of people. The Sunday Eucharist was full and grand with processions, choir, and servers filling the church. On Wednesday, I came to enjoy that we could usually all fit at once at the altar rail in the smaller chapel. After Easter, we made it our custom to worship on Sunday mornings, Wednesday middays, and to also make the Feasts of the church a priority: the Transfiguration, All Saints Day, and others.

The transition was not all smooth. Some in the pews on Sundays resisted our toddler worshipping with us when the church offered both a nursery and a children's church. We also had to reorder our lives to make church a priority. That shift was the one that changed our perspective the most. I learned how important discipline is to the life of faith.

My current rule of life says that I will take part in the Eucharist each Sunday and will also attend a midweek Eucharist whenever possible. Yes, I notice the "wiggle words" of "whenever possible" are more of a way out than is typical for the disciplines in my rule. I manage to worship most every week of the year in a Eucharist at least one day of the week, so I leave the commitment in place. My wife and I also pray the Daily Offices of Morning and Evening Prayer together, so that the Eucharist becomes a part of the ongoing turning, learning, and prayer of the Way of Love.

Reorienting Our Lives

When we worship, we place the Triune God at the center of our lives, offering adoration in response to what God has done in forming and redeeming all creation. Our word "worship" comes from the Old English *woerthship,* which meant to show the worth of someone or something. Worship meant to honor or revere and did not necessarily mean God. We still use the word for the way some fans "worship" Beyoncé or Lady Gaga. Worship is, however, mostly appropriately used for giving the honor due to God in praise, thanksgiving, and prayer.

I once happened entirely by accident upon a noon Eucharist in Bolivia, where I had been forced during a hopelessly bungled flight to Brazil. The day was absolute chaos, but stepping into that church for worship was a way of moving into another world. From the sunny sidewalk along the park in the main square with vendors along the street and taxis and other cars honking their horns for no discernable reason, I entered a quiet, intentional, beautiful space where a group gathered for the feast of a saint. No one knew that I had not even planned to be in the country that day. I did not know the burdens they carried or the joys they had shared.

They seemed to know each other as they exchanged the peace. It was like stepping into an Irish pub where the same group assembles day after day to share the same drinks and run through mostly the same conversation in a companionable way. I knew I stood out as a U.S. American, and yet I felt welcomed. I am sure the congregation was a part of that welcome. I recall smiles and handshakes. I recall the priest placing the host in my hand. Mostly, I felt that the true host knew I would be there all along, as if I had kept an appointment long in my planner. That realization helped me to reorient my life.

Not everything is about me, nor should it be. In worship, I acknowledge that and shift my focus from me at the center to God at the center. Committing myself to this as a discipline is not a chore, but a life-giving necessity.

CHAPTER 6

Bless

Megan Castellan

BLESS: Share faith and unselfishly give and serve

"Freely you have received; freely give."

—Matthew 10:8 (NIV)

Jesus called his disciples to give, forgive, teach, and heal in his name. We are empowered by the Spirit to bless everyone we meet, practicing generosity and compassion, and proclaiming the Good News of God in Christ with hopeful words and selfless actions. We can share our stories of blessing and invite others to the Way of Love.[1]

The spiritual practice of blessing is at once simple and demanding. Christ asks us to share what we know and what we have,

---

1. "Bless," Episcopal Church, https://www.churchpublishing.org/wayoflovebless.

but often, it takes engaging in this sharing in order to even begin to know what it is we might have.

I was in the car, riding out to Southside Virginia on a warm spring day. It was a month or so into my ordained ministry, and I was headed out with two of my lay leaders, both of whom had highly successful careers working for the military in Hampton Roads.

Our task that sunny day was to find a project for a domestic mission trip. These two men hoped we might find a way to establish a relationship with some organization and put the resources of our large coastal church to use. We just didn't quite know what that would look like.

As they were products of military culture, both of my partners were fond of plans, analytics, and directions. Bill had typed up an agenda for our day; it helpfully included a "debriefing period" after each meeting and a final "mission debrief" following the day. He and Tom went back and forth a bit over whether our selected center of operations (the car) was ideal for such a meeting or whether we should stop and find a meeting room. I, being about a month out of seminary, was entirely intimidated by these two. My assurance that "we would know the right project when we saw it" sounded a bit hollow even to my ears.

But off we went.

Virginia, like almost all American locales, is rich both in history and in division. The three of us were products of the military-industrial build-up on the coast and all its bounty. Our parish was one of the largest in the diocese and one of the original four parishes of Virginia, anyone there would cheerfully tell you. The original building had been knocked down and moved several miles inland in the 1950s, when Oceana NAS needed to expand their runways. So now it stood just off the highway, a complete replica of what everyone thought the original building had looked like—down to the colonial box pews, the bare windows, and the gold-etched commandments and creed behind the tiny cross on the altar. (It was 2008, and Virginia Beach's stately churches still had a healthy suspicion of "popery" and all things Catholic.)

We were a product of this story on that bright spring day, as we set out across the state. The narratives that shape us are not often conscious, but they are still real. About once a week, I had to gently remind someone that our building was about as historic as my mother. But that was Who We Were. We were historic, revered, and wealthy. We were the establishment, in our own eyes, and we preserved all that was good, noble, and true, as our ancestors had done before us.

The leaders of the parish felt, to their credit, that we should share what we had with our fellows, especially domestically. We had a food pantry program that was in the process of expanding. We were planning a mission relationship with the Anglican Church in Belize. Was there yet something else we could do in Virginia?

Our first stop that day was with the county free lunch program. The director wanted to make sure the children in her county still had access to food during the summer. "I really could use you," she said. "We need more hands." Her office was cluttered, and her desk was covered in papers—all the signs of a busy mind with so much to address, and not enough time or enough hands to do it.

Our final stop that day was St. Thomas Episcopal Church. It was a two-room cinderblock building, off a county highway in the scrub pines. A woman named Valerie, the matriarch of the parish, met us as we entered and regarded us with no small amount of bemusement. We traded pleasantries back and forth, until it became obvious that things were getting more awkward, not less. "Here's the question," I asked. "We have about fifteen volunteers and some money. If we gave you that, what could you do?"

Valerie didn't even blink. "We need a Vacation Bible School for kids in these parts. They go without food, most of them, and they forget reading and writing, and they run all about. If I get volunteers, I would have a Bible School. Teach the kids about Jesus, make sure they read and write, and someone talks to them during the summer."

Not missing a beat, she reached into her pocket. "I have a schedule I made up. Also, we have a van that all of us churches use to bring people who can't drive to church every week. We can get all the kids here to church if their parents work. I just need people. And some supplies. The rest I can do."

Out of the corner of my eye, I could see Bill's and Tom's mouths on the floor. I nodded and smiled, as Bill and Tom started to excitedly suggest Vacation Bible School volunteers who could help and things we could try. When we got back to the car, it was a foregone conclusion: we would be coming back in June to help carry out St. Thomas's Bible School.

It was a rousing success. Valerie corralled people from all over to help out at St. Thomas's. She knew everyone in the county, it seemed, and everyone showed up eventually. Their part-time priest came over, and we traded off the clergy duties as required. Tom's wife came up and baked with the kids. Valerie led the journal-writing, someone else led the reading segment, and every day was an adventure in figuring out how to work together and trust each other.

For Tom and Bill, my career-military compatriots, this was an exercise in flexibility. I worried, going into the week, that the real culture clash I had to worry about was between their love of explanatory spreadsheets, and Valerie's quiet, calm competence. Instead, what I discovered was how badly we needed to learn from and share blessing with each other.

As my crew discovered, St. Thomas's also had a rich narrative. It was founded by the Rev. James Solomon Russell, the first archdeacon of Southern Virginia and an incredible educator, preacher, and church planter, who founded thirty-eight black churches in Southside Virginia in the 1880s and 1890s. He also founded St. Paul's College, one of the Episcopal Church's few historically black colleges.

The descendants of those first worshippers at St. Thomas continue to worship there today, though the numbers have dwindled. Mostly it is two families on the rolls, but that is two *entire* families— generation down through generation, all branches included. The church is theirs, in a way that is tangible to feel when you walk in the doors, and in a way that is deeply moving. It is a place that feels loved.

The church was also the community's in a real way. Valerie explained the bus, in a later conversation. "No church around here has a pastor every Sunday, so we load up the van and go wherever has a pastor that week. Whether it's us or the Baptists or someone, we're all together, and we hear the Word."

Our narrative about where we came from was neat and tidy, but the longer we worked with St. Thomas, the more it became evident that our story had some holes we needed to struggle with. It failed to mention Rev. Russell, or his pioneering work, or the quiet, persistent, and pernicious segregation that had kept the Southside poor, and made certain sections of the coast rich. It failed to reckon with the troubling story of how, in 1953, the Confederate flag came to fly over the organ, and it failed to note how that flag effectively blocked any relationship with communities like St. Thomas's.

As our relationship with the people of Freeman strengthened, I found myself wrestling anew with all these truths. How might we use the whole of our privilege, as we uncovered it more and more, to bless others? Why had we built a narrative as a church that devalued so many of the gifts we now received from the people of St. Thomas's? It seemed the more we learned from each other, the more we discovered we could share with each other—and the greater transformation and vulnerability was required of us.

The spiritual practice of blessing seems easy at first. "Oh, yes," we think. "I can do this. I give to others out of my abundance. Not a problem!" We venture off to the thrift shop, the homeless shelter, the soup kitchen. We write checks, share fellowship. But, like all spiritual practices, if it is done with intention and prayer, the longer you engage in it, the deeper it will take you.

If you hand out sandwiches at a soup kitchen long enough, praying that you might be a blessing to those you encounter, sooner or later, you are going to start to wonder why and how people ended up in that food line to start with. If you offer some financial resources, you begin to ask how you came to have what you have, what others also have, and what difference our resources could make if we pooled and shared them. When you begin to get to know the people you seek to bless, then you discover that they are equally beloved and equally gifted children of God.

Blessing pulls you deeper. It requires you to see the other as an equal, neither perfect nor incomplete—just like you. The practice of blessing makes you curious about others' stories and encourages you to open the internal space to receive that gift. More than that, it draws you into one another's story, and you become a supporting character in their narrative. It teaches you to share the spotlight as it were, to no longer see everyone as players in your own drama, but to look for ways to advance their own well-being and flourishing.

Inevitably, this practice also leads the faithful Christian to confront some hard questions. As you honor the stories of others, and promote the abundant life that God intends for all of us, you also begin to recognize the systems and patterns that make your stories different in the first place. The practice of blessing does not allow you to remain at arm's length, but it leads you to question why the world is the way it is, and what God would have us do about it.

Blessing as an Act of Mutuality

There are lots of ways to share what God has given us with one another, once we learn to recognize it. We can give our financial resources, we can give our skills, we can give our time and our attention. Simone Weil once wrote that concentrated, dedicated attention is a pure form of prayer, and for so many people, having someone pay attention to them is a rare, beautiful thing. So paying attention to a person you usually overlook might be a place to begin, when you seek to practice blessing others. Listen to a child's endless story about their day. Watch the faces of the people you pass on the street. How are they feeling? Cultivate a sense of empathy and awareness the next time you are out and about, having everyday interactions with people. How can you pay absolute, undivided attention to them in that moment? As you go about your day, share your focus with others.

This is the perfect starting place, this cultivation of attention, because it counters our usual tendencies. So frequently when we endeavor to bless others, we begin not with what others need or even have, but what we want to share. Our focus is actually on ourselves, and not on others. In the Gospels, whenever Jesus Christ encounters someone who is troubled by demons or has an illness, he first asks "What would you like me to do for you?" Jesus doesn't presume to know what the person needs; he waits to be asked. He gives his attention and his presence to them, listens deeply to their stories and questions, and once that relationship is established, then they ask for what they need. Jesus—though the incarnate Son of God—doesn't force anything on anyone. The ways he blesses the people he encounters are mutual, and so they are life-giving.

Blessing also happens when we share our material resources. If you've ever tried to feed children, you've seen a basic example of how this works. The child who has more soon shares with the one who has less. We teach children about fairness and equity, and so they learn to share so everyone has enough.

In our world, some have more than others: more money, more talent, more resources. Those who have more can use those resources to contribute toward God's dream of a world where everyone has enough to live and to flourish. When you give freely of your skills and money in order to provide for others who have less, you challenge the idolatry of money in our lives. Christ calls us to give without counting the cost, and to give without strings attached, because the act of giving itself shapes us into disciples on the Jesus Way, and not followers after money. The more we let go of the resources the world insists are vital, the more we can learn to trust in God alone and seek after God's reign, rather than the illusory promises of our rampant consumer culture.

In my experience, blessing like this can lead seamlessly to the practice of Go: moving beyond our circles and comfort, witnessing to God's justice with our lips and our lives, listening with humility and forming Beloved Community.[2] If we find ourselves called to cross dividing lines and share blessing with specific people in a specific place, we may also be called to address the imbalance that led to this situation in the first place. Having formed genuine relationship, we may be inspired and energized to create a world where no one suffers lack at all.

Like all the practices in the Way of Love, blessing transforms both us *and* the world around us. As we learn to share with

2. See more about the practice of Go in chapter 7.

others—through service, evangelism, generosity, pastoral care, and healing and more—we also discover that God has equipped us abundantly. The more we bless others, the more we find we have to share, and the more need we see crying out before us. Blessing others, paying deep, profound attention to their needs and wants and gifts, sharing and receiving stories, draws us into their lives and experiences in a new way. It changes us, and it can change the world.

CHAPTER 7

Go

Robert Wright

GO: Cross boundaries, listen deeply, and live like Jesus

Jesus said to them . . . "Peace be with you. As the Father has sent me, so I send you."

—John 20:21

As Jesus went to the highways and byways, he sends us beyond our circles and comfort, to witness to the love, justice, and truth of God with our lips and with our lives. We go to listen with humility and to join God in healing a hurting world. We go to become Beloved Community, a people reconciled in love with God and one another.[1]

The Way of Love reaches the heights of its truthfulness and the depth of its usefulness in the principle of *go*.

---

1. "Go," Episcopal Church, https.//www.churchpublishing.org/wayof lovego.

Exhibit A of an active life with God is marked by a clear, calm, consistent, and expanding engagement with neighbor, community, and world. There are no two ways about it. Go is what Jesus asked us to do and who he asked us to be. Go into the world in his name by the power and aid of the Holy Spirit—that is the commission and covenantal agreement.

Before we go any further, so that we are clear, "go" is a verb meaning:

- **Move**, proceed, make one's way, advance, progress, pass; walk, travel, journey.
- **Extend**, stretch, reach, lead.
- **Leave**, depart, go away, withdraw, absent oneself, make an exit, exit: set off, start out, get underway, be on one's way; decamp, retreat, clear out, run off, make a move, make tracks, push off, skedaddle, scram, split, scoot.

"Go" for us means partnering with Jesus and his constantly enlarging neighbor-making campaign, especially as it leads us down into the fingernail-dirty places of the world. At least part of what Jesus means when he asks us to go, it seems, is go see how chock full of God the world is already.

Going is growing for us. The Way of Love in general and the practice of go in particular are a stretching exercise for the feet that benefits the heart, ours and others. What keeps us from wandering aimlessly on this grand adventure is a little help from our friends, namely Matthew, Mark, Luke, John, and Paul. Because of their life with Jesus and because of their faith experiences, you and I have reliable coordinates.

Going with God for the world puts us on a pathway that is broad and old, well-traveled and not nearly traveled enough. This pathway may lead us to church, but church is not the destination of the Way of Love. We don't hear in the Gospels that Jesus substituted world awareness and work for temple worship. In fact, he had some pointed things to say to people who had fallen into this trap. Pastor Greg Laurie captures this idea perfectly when he says, "Jesus did not say that the whole world should go to church, but He did say that the church should go to the whole world."[2]

There is a lot of anxiety in church about the future of the church (in a word, decline). There is anxiety about the loss of our mainstream American religious culture. There is anxiety and confusion about how to move from an edifice-based, membership-obsessed Christian faith into the walking, talking, power-demonstrating expression of God's love for the world that Jesus preached and modeled. Only a reclaimed and reenergized "go" imperative is adequate medicine for ecclesiastical anxiety. Only going into the world for his sake will give us a purpose, a future, and a hope.

"For God so loved the world. . . ." (John 3:16)

---

2. Greg Laurie, *Tell Someone: You Can Share the Good News* (Nashville: B&H Publishing Group, 2016).

Folks rush right by these five words on their way to God's generous act of giving Jesus to the world to save and offer life. What if we slowed down and focused on the first part of the verse: "For God so loved the world . . ."? If Luke's tenth chapter is a blueprint for *how* the followers of Jesus can engage the world, then the fact that God loves the world is the reason *why* we should engage the world. To love God is to love the things God loves. God loves the world, so we go to love it too.

I often ask groups what comes to mind when they hear talk about the world. I think about Jesus our founder. He was born under questionable circumstances to a nobody and a day laborer in a stable during the crush and messiness of a regional census. His parents suddenly greeted visitors who traveled from afar to see the holy infant born in scandal: fortune-telling foreigners, star-gazing, wandering elites from modern-day Iraq. They might have been "wise" men, but they were worrisome with all their reverence and predictions about a child born to a family from the ghetto.

Jesus's family would soon immigrate to Africa, because there was a death warrant out for them. During their time in Egypt, Joseph probably hired himself out for odd jobs and lived hand-to-mouth, just like the people who stand outside of Home Depot or Lowes nowadays do. Already you can see so much of "the world" in this story.

Meanwhile, we cut to Jesus's cousin John the Baptist, a good Jewish boy gone wild. He probably heard from his community, "you know you shouldn't take your religion so seriously." John's religion pointed him toward the world. He was finished with the incense and daily prayers of his father and mother. His feet wanted to be planted in the mud of the Jordan River, at the intersection of the sincere and the hypocrites. Remember, John is the preacher that set Jesus's heart on fire. All of this happened outside the walls of any sanctuary. All of this in the world.

Jesus follows the same pattern. You will notice that while he visits the temple occasionally, he saved the greatest part of his time and allegiance for those in the world, beyond the reach of the temple. If we are to be his church here and now, that same spirit will have to increase in us.

God is on a mission. God doesn't owe any particular church or denomination any preferential treatment based on the beauty of our vestments, architecture, liturgy, or tradition. Jesus is endowing and sending people into the world. Jesus is enlarging the circle of neighborliness. Jesus is teaching us to rely on each other and the strong arms of God's never-failing embrace. Jesus is launching a search-and-rescue mission for souls amidst the wolves of the world, and he is looking for partners in this enterprise. We can't help ourselves. We Go.

> After this the Lord appointed seventy others and sent them
> on ahead of him in pairs to every town and place where he
> himself intended to go. (Luke 10:1)

Jesus added seventy people from Galilee to his original twelve disciples. He appointed them. The word for appointed in Greek is *anede txen*, which means "to show clearly, to indicate; to lift up and present the one(s) who have been chosen; to proclaim someone as having been elected to an office." Appointed has to do with time, as in one is present at an agreed upon or even preordained time. You might also use the word "appointed" in terms of decorating. One's home or hotel room could be described as well appointed, furnished, and equipped.

These seventy people were chosen by Jesus and appointed for a particular time, decorated with a clear purpose and amply equipped with divine companionship and a transcendent peace. For Christians, being baptized is the clearest illustration that God has appointed us in Jesus's name, through the power of the Holy Spirit. To begin actually baptizing people, we tell the awesome story of God, water, and the world. We ask God to bless the water we are about to use in this initiation, then we splash water on an infant, teenager, or adult with these words "in the name of the Father, Son and Holy Spirit." This has been going on for two thousand years, which proves that we believe there is something in this solemn act. We are baptized, just like Jesus, just like St. Francis, just like Sister Helen Prejean, just like Grandma, just like the little one who isn't even alive now but will be baptized next All Saints.

We then smear oil on the newly baptized person's forehead, and say, "You are sealed by the Holy Spirit in Baptism and marked as Christ's own forever." We don't baptize in secret, but in front of God, family, friends, and guests. It is clear to all who are present that someone has been elected and commissioned. It's like Jesus is showing off the latest members of his movement, God's movement.

To be appointed by God, in Jesus's name through the power of the Holy Spirit, is an immense privilege. As every ambassador knows, this is the privilege of going on behalf of a greater and more glorious whole. I encourage you to pause now and take this in. The creator of all the worlds has appointed you to go to the places God is already, to confirm for others that God is still in the reaching-out and resurrection business. You are to confirm for the world that love is the most durable thing in the world, and you can do so with joy!

Appointment by God is time-specific. Archbishop Tutu has said, in his delightfully impish way, "There are no accidents in God, though some of us might look like an accident."[3] You and I are here and now, with all the blessings and challenges that entails. God wanted us here and now. We are fearfully and wonderfully made.

I like the thought of that. We are not flotsam and jetsam in the river of time floating arbitrarily. We are here in this millennium, this century, this decade, this year, month, and day because we are *supposed* to be here. "Like arrows in the hands of a warrior," as Psalm 127 puts it, we have been shot into now. We were not meant to be contemporaries of Moses, Miriam, or Martin Luther King Jr. We were meant to be fully here, living out our faith at a time when the church is ebbing in some places and lurching forward in others.

Believing in Jesus here and now sometimes may feel like we are on a rickety raft of good news in an vast ocean of heinous news: police shootings, the prison industrial complex, wars based on knowingly false intelligence, gun violence, anti-immigration sentiment by the very people who depend most on immigrant labor; the death of

---

3. Desmond Tutu, *God Has a Dream: A Vision of Hope for Our Time* (New York: Doubleday, 2004), 41–42.

children all over the world by poverty and suicide. All in addition to racism, sexism, homophobia, and greed.

Like Esther, the young wife of King Xerxes, you and I have been appointed "for such a time as this." And while the odds seem insurmountable, that has been true for every generation of Jesus's followers. Like a tree planted by the riverside drawing nutrients up from down deep, we are planted here to bloom and to be tangible evidence that there is a God and this God has come close in Jesus Christ. We are the proof to this generation that God is not deaf or indifferent.

God has actually paid us a great compliment by putting us here at this great transitional moment in the life of faith. Somehow in deep collusion with all that is wrong with our present age, we are also the people suited to help God turn the world right-side-up by following Jesus now. And so we go, because that is what we were appointed to do.

> A sent ministry is a countercultural challenge. It's the subordination of your career, marriage, and family, and even the choice of where to sleep at night. . . . [It]'s weirdly un-American. We are a people who have been deeply indoctrinated into the godless ideology that our lives are our possessions to do with as we please, that my life is the sum of my astute choices, and that the life I'm living is my own.[4]

---

4. William Willimon, "Sent: An Ordination Sermon," Day 1, June 7, 2012, https://day1.org/articles/5d9b820ef71918cdf20031cf/bishop_william _willimon_sentan_ordination_sermon.

Just as we hear about the appointment of seventy new followers of Jesus, he tells us they were also "sent." He sends them "ahead of him to towns and places he intends to go himself." No cookies. No punch. No probationary period. No apprenticeship. Just go. I need you out there, doing my work, being my message.

The proximity of those two words—appointed and sent—indicates to me that they go together in Jesus's mind. Christians are appointed for motion.

That is not an affirmation to live a frenzied life. Christian sent-ness is a call for purposeful, prayerful movement. It is a call to go where Jesus himself intended to go. You might say we are supposed to be on our way somewhere for no other reason than Jesus told us to go there. Listening for and living into that is the stuff of spiritual maturity.

Understanding sent-ness as faithfulness is first about how we understand our life. In other words, to whom does our life belong? This is countercultural wisdom. Embracing being sent is first about understanding Jesus's lordship over our lives. Faith is generally about believing in God and Jesus. If we say the right words, give assent to right ideas, then we are followers of Jesus. Or believing is being a good person who does good things and runs good errands for God. These understandings do not quite reach the radical notion of belonging to God that produces radical sent-ness.

Think about Jesus and Mary his mother. Each said virtually the same thing in response to overtures and opportunities afforded by God. Mary said to the angel Gabriel, "Let it be unto me according to thy word." Jesus said to God as he wept in the garden of Gethsemane,

"Not my will but thy will be done." In both of their lives—as well as in the lives of Noah, Sarah, Miriam, Moses, Jacob, Esther, Naomi, Joseph, Isaiah, and really too many people to list—miracles happen because they understand themselves as belonging to God.

There is something else about living the sent life. If we return to William Willimon's sermon on being sent: "[F]orgive me for thinking [that there are] few more adventuresome ways [to live] than a life commandeered by Jesus into sent ministry."[5] There it is, in one wonderful word: adventuresome. Baptized people are appointed and sent toward adventure. Here is what that familiar word really means:

1. an unusual and exciting, typically hazardous, experience or activity.
2. *synonyms*: exploit, escapade, deed, feat, experience.

The word "adventure" holds together two ideas: that something is about to happen *and* to arrive. In other words, something will happen as we are arriving. That is why Jesus sent the seventy ahead of him, so they could see the stuff that happens when you arrive as good news.

The apostle Paul is the poster child for Christian adventure. In the book of Acts and through his many letters, you see Paul on the move. Whether he remains in a city for a couple of years or if he is just passing through, Paul is on a Jesus-inaugurated adventure to engage, inspire, and equip people with all that he knows about God in Jesus. Here are some of his adventures:

---

5. Ibid.

[I]imprisonments, with countless floggings, and often near death. Five times I have received from the Jews the forty lashes minus one. Three times I was beaten with rods. Once I received a stoning. Three times I was shipwrecked; for a night and a day I was adrift at sea; on frequent journeys, in danger from rivers, danger from bandits, danger from my own people, danger from Gentiles, danger in the city, danger in the wilderness, danger at sea, danger from false brothers and sisters; in toil and hardship, through many a sleepless night, hungry and thirsty, often without food, cold and naked. And, besides other things, I am under daily pressure because of my anxiety for all the churches. . . . In Damascus, the governor under King Aretas guarded the city of Damascus in order to seize me, but I was let down in a basket through a window in the wall, and escaped from his hands. (2 Cor. 11:23–28, 32–33)

One thing is certain: Paul and his band of believers took their faith on the road. Their faith led them to and on adventure. The status quo will not deliver to us the adventure God begs us to embark on. And if we are uncertain whether we want to sign up, listen again to Willimon:

[F]ew things [are] sadder than an unsent life. What a joy, in good times, but especially in bad, to believe that you are where you are because you have been put there, and you are doing what you are doing because God means for this to be so. In a sense, we believe that every follower of Jesus Christ, clergy or not, is sent.[6]

The unsent life, the play-it-safe life, holds tremendous and awful consequences for us. First, there is the tragedy of insights never gained or the intimacy never shared with Jesus, because *out there* is where we could really hear his whispers and feel his abiding presence. *Out there* is where we experience the reliance and peace that come because we offer our whole selves to God in adventure. When there is no adventure to our faith, phrases like "radical reliance on God" and "peace that passes understanding" remain far away details of someone else's story. As Martin Luther King Jr. once observed:

> You may be thirty-eight years old, as I happen to be. And one day, some great opportunity stands before you and calls you to stand up for some great principle, some great issue, some great cause. And you refuse to do it because you are afraid. . . . You refuse to do it because you want to live longer. . . . You're afraid that you will lose your job, or you are afraid that you will be criticized or that you will lose your popularity, or you're afraid that somebody will stab you, or shoot at you or bomb your house; so you refuse to take the stand. Well, you may go on and live until you are ninety, but you're just as dead at thirty-eight as you would be at ninety.

6. Willimon, "Sent."

And the cessation of breathing in your life is but the belated announcement of an earlier death of the spirit.[7]

The world misses out on so much—and we miss out on so much—when you and I keep the ships of our lives in safe harbors.

Those who find their life will lose it, and those who lose their life for my sake will find it. (Matt. 10:39)

All this is true. Something also needs to be said about the risk associated with going and bearing the compassion of Jesus. We know from the Bible that Jesus's way of life was a risky undertaking, for him and for everyone who followed him. If you and I are going to do today what Jesus commends, we're going to find ourselves at the intersection of risk, even danger, and compassion.

When last did you find yourself at that intersection? I remember the first time I visited a prison alone. I was a young seminarian. I had done my due diligence. I had been coached by a seasoned prison chaplain as to how things should go. I spent weeks shadowing him. Now it was my turn. I had my Bible and that was it. I was, I thought, where Jesus would have me to be that day. The truth is I was scared. I was to be let loose in "general population." By my count, more than fifty inmates and me. What to say? How to be? Should anything

---

7. Martin Luther King Jr., "But If Not" (sermon, Ebenezer Baptist Church Atlanta, Georgia, November 1967).

have gone wrong, it would have taken the guards quite a while to get to me. I was sure they could smell the fear on me.

There I was, at the intersection of danger and compassion. I only remember two things about that visit. One, the loud metal on metal bang of the cell door slamming behind me. Two, the conversation I had with a young man behind a door. He was really just a boy. He was locked up for his own safety. He had shot and killed someone, but now, he found himself surrounded by hardened criminals, and he had no gun. He asked if I would pray for him and if I would remember him. I did.

That was not the first time I let my faith take me places that I feared. Like many things, practice makes perfect (or at least makes easier). Maybe the places that cause us the most fear are the places we are most needed. Maybe the places that strike us as grotesque or beneath our station in life are precisely where we ought to pay a visit. Are there any places you are afraid to visit?

Of course, in all of this, I am not asking anyone to be careless. I am certainly not asking anyone to place their life at risk naively. I am saying the opposite. What I hope and commend is an informed and strategic movement of compassion. Compassion cannot just be a feeling. Compassion, in the best sense of the word, has got to be the rocket fuel that shoots us beyond selflessness, through our legitimate fears, alongside of people who are most vulnerable. I think that is what Jesus means when he says, "Those who find their life will lose it, and those who lose their life for my sake will find it."

Blessed, Broken, and Sent

So we go to the most vulnerable, to the risky places, sometimes just to show up and practice the ministry of presence. There are times where simply being present counts for everything: at the death bed, on death row, with young children. But ours is not simply a ministry of presence. Going forth to love God and neighbor according to Jesus's gospel is an active undertaking. It is participating with God in relieving some distress, in healing and making whole.

We, like bread, are taken, blessed, broken, and distributed. You and I are the beneficiaries of God's love and mercy in the person of Jesus coming among us. God essentially left a gated community called heaven and came to us. In Jesus, God risked rejection, scorn, and death. You and I are the beneficiaries of the Holy Spirit, who swirls ahead of us and under us, giving us the power and buoyancy to be the partners in mission with God.

We go into the world for Christ because that is who we are and not simply what we do. We go because to live any other way would not be life for us, it would only be existing. By the grace of God, through word and story, song and worship, joy and pain, with neighbor and stranger, you and I may one day realize this is our highest calling: going on God's behalf into the world God loves.

CHAPTER 8

Rest

William Lupfer and Peter Elliott

REST: Receive the gift of God's grace, peace, and restoration

Peace I leave with you; my peace I give you. I do not give to you as the world gives. Do not let your hearts be troubled, and do not be afraid.

—John 14:27

From the beginning of creation, God has established the sacred pattern of going and returning, labor and rest. Especially today, God invites us to dedicate time for restoration and wholeness—within our bodies, minds, and souls, and within our communities and institutions. By resting, we place our trust in God, the primary actor who brings all things to their fullness.

Thus the heavens and the earth were finished, and all their multitude. And on the seventh day God finished the work that he had done, and he rested on the seventh day from all the work that he had done. So God blessed the seventh day and hallowed it, because on it God rested from all the work that he had done in creation.

—Genesis 2:1–3

In the creation story in Genesis, God creates the heavens and earth at breakneck speed. It's wondrous and mysterious. The story of creation opens our minds to the breadth of the cosmos, the depth of the oceans, the wild diversity of life. God's energy in creation is exceptional, relentless.

And then, on the seventh day—nothing: God does nothing. God simply rests—there is no purpose in the activity but to stop doing and enjoy what has been done. It is the Sabbath. Later in Scripture a day of rest becomes one of the Ten Commandments. It's that important.

Creation and rest are joined in God's creative act. As God created all that is, God creates the seventh day as a day of rest. God actually *creates* rest. God offers rest to the whole creation as an essential aspect of life. Rest is a gift from God and is offered to each of us as a blessing.

Not only is rest God's gift, rest is the pinnacle of God's creation. Biblical scholar John Dominic Crossan proposes that the Genesis account of creation all heads to this moment, where God rests.[1] Just

---

1. John Dominic Crossan, "Lecture 2: Covenantal Law: Human Destiny or Divine Sanction," *The Character of the Covenantal God: Toward a Christian Theology of the Christian Bible*, Borg-Crossman Seminars, June 18, 2013, http://johndominiccrossan.com/Lectures/Borg-Crossan/06-18-13/Lecture%202.pdf.

like a good joke heads to the punch line at the end of a story, the many lists in the Bible are heading to the main point. In the Genesis account, there is a list of eight acts of creation, squeezed into six days. On the seventh day, God rested and blessed and hallowed it as a day of rest forever. End of list.

Sabbath rest is for the whole creation, beginning with the creator, including the human ones, the animals, even the fields. The human ones, created in the divine image, are therefore charged to imitate the divine by also resting, and by ensuring that the creation also rests.

Sabbath rest is a weekly reminder that it's not all up to us. Author and priest Barbara Brown Taylor describes how, after she left parish ministry, she discovered an authentic practice of Sabbath:

> While Mishnah and Talmud go into great detail about what may or may not be done on the Sabbath, Torah is very straightforward: you shall not do any work. The key, for me, was freedom from compulsion. One day a week, "should," "ought" and "must" had no power over me. On Sundays I did not worship the clock, the dollar or my superego. I worshiped God instead, whom I trusted to run the world for one day without my help. I cannot even bring myself to tell you how I spent those days, since my mind still calls it sloth.
>
> It was not sloth. It was sabbath, and its effect was immediate. Relationships became more spacious. Prayer became more spacious. Time itself became more spacious. Instead of charging out of the gate on Monday mornings, I found myself sauntering instead, still relishing the freedom of the

day before. There was never enough time to get everything done, but I finally understood there never would be. There would only be enough time to live, with as much gratitude as I could muster.[2]

We don't have to fix everything, and we can't control most anything. When we take the time, we can discover the God who calls us to join in the divine action of rest. We can receive the blessing of rest.

Receiving the Blessing of Rest

The earth is the LORD's and all that is in it,
the world, and those who live in it. —Psalm 24:1

Can you remember the first time you rested in God? For me (Bill), it happened in Northern Canada, along the Missinaibi River in Ontario. I was with a group of sixteen-year-olds on a several-week, 350-mile canoe trip with two college-age counselors. About two-thirds of the way on our journey, we paused and entered a three-day "solo." One counselor got out of the canoe and we paddled downriver, dropping a camper off every half mile until the final leader made camp, a half-mile downstream from the final camper. Each camper made a rudimentary camp without tent or food and just . . . rested.

---

2. Barbara Brown Taylor, "Letting God Run Things without My Help," *The Christian Century,* May 5, 1999, https://www.christiancentury.org /article/2011-12/remember-sabbath.

My three-day solo was a combination of extreme boredom, fear (I imagined a bear was nearby, only to find out later that a bear had indeed raided our food stash a half-mile downstream), and spiritual insight. I first gave in to my exhaustion and slept as much as I could. A day and a half later, I crawled out of my sleeping bag and began to explore the river. I found my way through the brush to the rocky riverbank and drank the clean river water. By now, the river was a half-mile wide, full and fresh. I drank to assuage my thirst. Then I drank to assuage my hunger.

Restored from exhaustion, I began to ponder. Upriver from me were a bunch of kids a year older than I, many of whom were friends from previous summers at camp. Each had come to faith in their own ways during the previous years. Over the past two weeks we had spent many hours in the canoes by day and around the campfire by night, discussing our faith. Surrounded by this community, I had remained silent. I wasn't sure about God and had never had an experience of God's presence.

As I sat alone in silence watching the waters flow, I wondered how the river replenished itself. It wasn't raining, and few rivers flowed into the Missinaibi. The clean, drinkable water flowed with abundance and it began to dawn on me, next to this magical river that had a strong personality, indeed, a soul, that there was no way I could disprove the existence of God. It made sense for me to look for God in my life, my friends, the world around me, and in my own soul.

That insight proved to be the instance of my conversion.

There were no bells or whistles. No visions. No comforting words from Jesus. No slaking of my extreme hunger. Not even a change in my mental habits. The only thing that changed for me was that I discovered a commitment, excavated from the depth of my soul, that I was ready, indeed committed, to enter the threshold of a spiritual adventure. I would seek God's presence.

I didn't tell anyone about the experience. It was too new. I didn't have words for what happened, but the conversion was confirmed for me when I returned home after camp. Immediately, without explaining myself, I changed everything in my life: my friends, my reading, my habits, my intentions. It was startling for me and others who knew me.

Reflecting back now, I can see that my consciousness was opened by intentional rest, set in a community of supportive relationships that were developed over time. Through rest in God's creation, I came to know and experience God.

Over the years since, I have heard many people describe their primary experience of God in creation. We discover the Creator in creation, the first authentic revelation of God (Scripture is the second). Some experience God in the power and might of the ocean. For others, a quiet stream prompts contemplation and a sense of peace. Working in a garden, climbing a mountain, watching a bird at a feeder—in creation we discover there is something bigger than ourselves, something other than ourselves: a mystery and a certainty at once. Resting in creation requires us to stop the busyness of our daily lives and foster attentiveness to God's presence around us.

Rest is the doorway that opens in our soul and allows God to enter. God enters when we give up control and simply open the door to wonder. When we begin to wonder about the beauty of the earth and its oneness, we are inspired to join in God's work of making justice for the earth and all its people. But it all begins in rest.

Radical Rest Gets Jesus in Trouble

> He said to them, "Come away to a deserted place all by yourselves and rest a while." For many were coming and going, and they had no leisure even to eat. —Mark 6:31

Because it's not always possible to retreat deep into God's creation to find rest, generations of faithful people have found ways to bring rest into everyday life. In the process, rest has been surrounded with ritualized protection and boundaried practice: take a nap on a Sunday, observe a brief silence after a Scripture reading in worship, go on a family vacation. The rest that was once wild and free and built into the heart of creation has been domesticated. As Aidan Kavanagh once said, "[W]e have allowed ourselves to tame the Lion of Judah and put him into a suburban zoo to entertain children."[3]

Jesus did not domesticate rest. Jesus's soul sent him into rest whenever his ministry required, not according to a liturgical timetable. Jesus defied expectations of when and how to rest, leaving the crowds just as they were clamoring for him, with so many still needing to be fed and to be healed. Even his disciples often could

---

3. Aidan Kavanagh, *On Liturgical Theology: The Hale Memorial Lectures of Seabury-Western Theological Seminary* (Collegeville, MN: Liturgical Press, 1984), 94.

not understand how he could walk away from the demanding and deserving crowds.

In his book *Sabbath*, Wayne Muller uses plants to make a distinction between two stages of dormancy: *quiescence*, or when a plant slows in response to environmental cues, such as colder weather, and *rest*, which is controlled not from without, but from within. In his example, during rest, a plant heeds its inner clock, and emerges only in the fullness of time.[4]

When Jesus left the crowds to pray, he was not seeking a weekend with friends. He was not leaving to replenish his depletion. Today, we treat rest as a necessary evil, an antidote to exhaustion—we rest when we can't do any more or go any further, and our goal is to fill up the gas tank so we can continue whatever it is we're doing. We rest only in order to not be tired.

Unlike most of us, Jesus rested to relate to God. Jesus rested to bask in the presence of the One who loved him completely. His rest gave him what he needed to love others as God loved them, to see God in them, to serve God through them. As Muller says:

> So when we see Jesus withdraw from the press of the crowds and retreat to a place of rest, he is not simply taking a well-deserved break from his useful but exhausting ministry. He

---

4. Wayne Muller, *Sabbath: Finding Rest, Renewal, and Delight in Our Busy Lives* (New York: Bantam Books, 1999), 58.

is honoring a deep spiritual need for a time dedicated not to accomplishment and growth, but to quiescence and rest.[5]

What would it look like if we approached rest the same way—as a time to feel enveloped in the love of God? Not as physical replenishment, but as spiritual grounding? If we are to walk in the way of love, we must take time to rest deeply in the presence of the One whose love is the ground of being.

Every Day Is Sabbath

Remember the Sabbath day, and keep it holy. —Exodus 20:8

Rest is so important to our spiritual health, our forebears understood it as a commandment. The commandment to keep a holy Sabbath was meant not just to provide a respite from the daily tasks of survival, but to clear away the distractions from our spiritual life. The purpose of Sabbath is to create a time and space for us to make space for God in our lives and for us to rest in God.

Jesus did not ignore the Sabbath. He radicalized it. He rescued it from its ritual container and enjoyed purposeful, meaningful rest every day.

Today, there are movements around various types of Sabbath—you can take a tech Sabbath, a social media Sabbath, a news Sabbath. All are responses to a sense of feeling overwhelmed by the sheer

---

5. Ibid.

volume of information and opinions that come to our devices. In some ways these movements are similar to the commandment to keep a holy Sabbath, which also requires us to eliminate distractions. But Sabbath is defined not just by what we do without; it's what we do *with* the space and time we are creating.

It is difficult to just stop, because so much inside us compels us to keep going: to check our devices, to respond to that e-mail, to write that sermon, to make that phone call. Our little minds cycle round to find "something to do," perhaps because simply being still can leave us feeling anxious. I have found that moving slowly toward rest helps; beginning with taking a Sabbath moment, then a Sabbath hour, a Sabbath half-day. Perhaps it begins with going on an hour-long walk and leaving your phone behind. The important thing is to make time each day for rest, to stop, to be still, and to be in touch with God.

A prayer group I was once part of began each session with the phrase, "Be still and know that I am God." But we said it in a very particular way. First we said the whole sentence, "Be still and know that I am God." Then we said, "Be still and know." Then, "Be still." Finally, "Be." And then we sat in silence for twenty minutes.

It's all about learning how to "Be."

Rest in Jesus

Come to me, all you that are weary and are carrying heavy burdens, and I will give you rest. Take my yoke upon you, and learn from me; for I am gentle and humble in heart, and you will find rest for your souls. For my yoke is easy, and my burden is light. —Matthew 11:28–30

When in prayer and worship we seek to draw close to Jesus, we discover that the way of love includes a gentle invitation to rest. Jesus's invitation is to abundant life—not to frenetic existence or overbooked schedules. A key ingredient in that abundance is rest for our souls. How do we find this rest? Here are three practical suggestions:

Make Time

The biblical notion of Sabbath is one day in seven for rest. In a 24/7 North American culture, this can be hard to achieve. If you're a parent, you're often ferrying your children to events or practices. If you're clergy, there are people who need your attention and there are tasks to accomplish every day. Couples who each have a work life often have schedules that keep them going seven days a week. Perhaps you could look at your calendar for a two-month period and schedule at least one day in seven to take a break—including ignoring your devices—and simply rest. Or perhaps there's a spiritual retreat offered by your parish or diocese and you could commit to that as a time to rest.

Focus on Your Breathing

In his book *The Naked Now*, Richard Rohr reminds us that the Jewish name for God—Yahweh—was not spoken, but breathed. Its correct pronunciation is an attempt to imitate the sound of inhalation and exhalation. We do that every moment: our first and last word as we enter and leave the world. The one thing we do every moment of our lives is therefore to speak the name of God. Taking some time every day to simply focus on your breath, to use God's holy name Yah-weh: "Yah," as you breathe in, and "weh" as you breathe out, slows down your incessant mental chatter and can leave you calmer, having rested in God's name. Or you can use the name Jesus in the same way; breathing in "Je . . ." and out ". . . sus."[6]

Calm Your Mind

Consider using this verse from Scripture: "You are my . . . beloved; with you I am well pleased" (Mark 1:11). This verse is part of the Gospel account of the baptism of Jesus. When he comes out of the water, a voice from heaven is heard to say, "You are my beloved. . . ." When we are baptized, we are joined with him in his baptism and share through God's grace the privilege of being the beloved ones of God. As Henri Nouwen writes:

> Yes, there is that voice, the voice that speaks from above and from within and that whispers softly or declares loudly: "You are my Beloved, on you my favor rests." It certainly is not easy to hear that voice in a world filled with voices that shout: "You are no good, you are ugly; you are worthless;

---

6. Richard Rohr, *The Naked Now: Learning to See as the Mystics See* (New York: Crossroads Publishing, 2009), 25–26.

you are despicable, you are nobody—unless you can demonstrate the opposite."[7]

To rest in Christ is to know yourself as beloved, and from that knowledge to be an instrument of the way of love in the world.[8]

The Value of Rest

So then, a sabbath rest still remains for the people of God; for those who enter God's rest also cease from their labors as God did. . . . Let us therefore make every effort to enter that rest. —Hebrews 4:9–11

The letter to the Hebrews invites us to make every effort to enter into the rest of God. Ceasing from labors, taking the creative pause, being open to experience God in nature, listening for the movement of the Spirit in music. Consider these and many other ways to enter rest, God's gift to us. As Muller writes:

The currency that gives birth to love is time. All love grows in time. When we live without taking time for love to grow,

---

7. Henri Nouwen, *Life of the Beloved: Spiritual Living in a Secular World* (New York: Crossroads Publishing, 1992), 31.
8. If you need more inspiration for rest, see Rhett Parker's online article "A Day of Rest: 12 Scientific Reasons It Works" or Brené Brown's list of "Ten Guideposts for Wholehearted Living," in *Rising Strong: How the Ability to Reset Transforms the Way We Live, Love, Parent, and Lead.*

there is only a thin veneer of what we really are looking for. The depth of the love we seek requires time to work in us. Most spiritual traditions counsel that Sabbath time isn't a lifestyle suggestion for your blood pressure, it's a commandment. Rest. You must stop your work and allow yourself to be worked on by time.[9]

This is the goal: to be worked on in time so the depth of love can grow in us. We cannot be practitioners of the way of love unless we open the gracious space for this work to unfold in us. After all, the Christian life is not only about "doing," it is also about "being."

To live a Jesus-centered life is to seek to imitate him in our lives today. As a keeper of the Jewish Sabbath, Jesus would have been aware of wisdom expressed more recently by Rabbi Abraham Heschel, who said, "There is a realm of time where the goal is not to have but to be, not to own but to give, not to control but to share, not to subdue but to be in accord. Life goes wrong when the control of space, the acquisition of things of space, becomes our sole concern."[10]

This realm of time that Sabbath seeks to inculcate in the lives of faithful people is indeed what Jesus referred to as "eternal life." It propels us to a way of being, not doing; of giving, not owning, of sharing, not controlling. It beautifully summarizes the Way of Love—the Way that is undergirded by our rest.

---

9. Wayne Muller, *Sabbath: Finding Rest, Renewal, and Delight in Our Busy Lives* (New York: Bantam Books, 1999), 58.

10. Abraham Joshua Heschel, *Sabbath: Its Meaning for Modern Man* (New York: Farrar, Straus and Giroux, 1951), 3.

Why Jesus and His Way of Love?

Stephanie Spellers

I n its own way, each chapter of this book has answered an essential question about the Way of Love. What is a Rule of Life? What are these seven spiritual practices? How do we take each practice seriously, as individual followers of Jesus and as leaders of Christian community?

As we conclude the book and bless one another for the journey, I find one more question continues to percolate: *why?* In a world full of choices and pathways, why should we turn and learn, pray and worship, bless and go, and at last rest? Why would we weave these practices into a coherent whole and form small circles of fellow travelers who share the commitment? Why center our lives on Jesus, as compared to some other wise teacher or deep purpose? Why do we believe following the Way of Love makes any difference in our lives or the life of the whole church?

I regularly hear this "why?" from people who've been in church their whole lives, many of them suspicious of anything that smells like the latest Christian fad. I hear the "why?" from friends who have nothing to do with church and feel just fine crafting beautiful, even spiritual, yet distinctly nonreligious lives. When I get quiet enough, this "why?" is waiting at the core of my own being: "Stephanie, what are you seeking and why do you believe you're going to find it on this Way with this Jesus?"

In the Beginning

Two thousand years ago, simple folk moved about the Ancient Near East with similar questions and hopes. Some of them latched onto John the Baptist, peppering him with their questions and expectations. "Are you the Messiah? The prophet? The one we've been waiting for?" Then one day Jesus walked by. John pointed at him and said, "Look, here is the Lamb of God. All the things you're coming to me for, you'll find with him. Now go!" So they went (John 1:19–36).

When Jesus turned and saw two of John's followers now on his tracks, he asked: "What are you looking for?" Their answer: "Rabbi (Teacher), where are you staying?" In other words, "We want to learn from you and to see how you live and where you dwell. We've been staying with John, eating wild locusts and honey and chafing under our hair shirts. Maybe we could come with you?"

I can see Jesus's winsome, wry smile as he offered the invitation, "Come and see." They came. They saw. And according to John 1:39, "they remained with him that day" . . . and presumably for many days to come.

Have you ever wondered what they saw? What was he doing, what was he radiating, that made them stick around? I believe—and several of his first disciples eventually proclaimed—that they saw the fullness of God drawn near to dwell in our midst. The sheer power of that presence changed their lives and changed the world.

Why do I follow him? Why am I so passionate about seeing Episcopalians everywhere taking up intentional discipleship along the Way of Love, and why do I long to share this path with people who usually run screaming from the very mention of Christianity? Because in Jesus, God shows up close enough for us to taste, smell, hold, see, ingest, and even become. Looking at him, we see what God looks like. Living like him, dwelling with him, following him as Teacher and growing in loving relationship with him, we become more fully God's body alive in the world.

The Way of Love, like any rule of life, essentially describes Jesus's life and then invites us to lovingly shape our lives around his.

- Why do we turn? Jesus *turned* toward God. Approaching the cross with tears, he surely could have found some way out. Instead he prayed, "Father . . . not my will but yours be done" (Luke 22:42).
- Why do we learn? Jesus *learned* about God from the Scriptures. From his youth, he opened the holy books and communed with the God of Israel whose voice and teachings he found there (Luke 2:40–52).

- Why pray? Jesus *prayed* to God constantly, in wonder, in hope, in pain, in adoration, in thanksgiving. His whole life was a prayer to the God who was and is his Abba and companion (Matt. 6:9–13).

- Why worship? Jesus *worshiped* in the temple. Even as he promised that he could tear it down and build it right back up again, even as he tore through with a whip of cords, the temple and the true worship it was supposed to host were vital to Jesus's life (Matt. 21:12–13).

- Why bless? Jesus *blessed* with every moment, giving his life away as an offering to God because he knew he'd get even more life back (Mark 8:35).

- Why on earth would we go? Jesus's life was the very definition of *go*. How often he traveled to the edge and stood in solidarity with sinners and tax collectors (Mark 2:15–18), women and children (Matt. 9:18–26), and all manner of unsavory characters that he knit together in one of the world's first Beloved Communities.

- Why rest? Jesus *rested*, sometimes getting up early to have quiet time with God (Mark 1:35) and sometimes snoozing in the stern of a boat on storm-tossed sea (Mark 4:35–40). He regularly carved out moments when he placed the world and his own life in the hands of his Father God.

Why follow Jesus in his Way of Love? Because Jesus lived a whole life rooted in love for God and spreading out in love and honor for every person and encounter that followed (Matt. 22:3–40). He holds that life out to us. He promised that if we stay with him and follow his teachings, we would find he lives in us, and we in him (John 15). In the Way of Love, we're taking him at his word and finding it to be true.

We Seek Love, Freedom, and Abundant Life

Why follow Jesus in his Way of Love? What are we hoping to find? Indeed, what are we finding? We humans aren't especially complicated creatures. What did those first disciples want? What do most human beings still want? To be loved, to be free, to experience life in its fullness. I wonder if this is what is happening for the thousands of Episcopalians taking up Jesus's Way of Love and for our friends throughout the Anglican Communion who are also committing to intentional discipleship and "Jesus-shaped Life."[1] We are recalling the loving, liberating, life-giving promise of Jesus, and in him we're discovering more of love, freedom, and abundant life.

These spiritual gifts have been present in the life of the church all along. Since 2017, it seems we are coming to a more intense, collective awareness of what we most yearn for and how taking up Jesus's Way of Love fulfills those longings.

---

1. Learn more about the Anglican Communion's Season of Intentional Discipleship and Jesus-Shaped Life at https://www.anglicancommunion.org/mission/intentional-discipleship.aspx.

We seek love . . . to know God's love, to love and be loved by others, and to love ourselves. (The Way of Love introductory brochure, part 1a)

Every time we open and *learn* from Scripture and every time we worship, we have the chance to fall more and more in love with God. Bible stories testify time and again to God's unfathomable love. I experience the reality and power of that love when I take in sanctified bread and wine. Love grows in me whenever I find myself worshiping with people radically different from me and discover something of God that I love in them too. And the more I hear the depth of God's love for me in Holy Scripture and in worship, I can say with conviction, "If God loves me, who am I not to love me too?"

To *pray* is to nurture loving relationship. I abide with God who is always and already present to me. Sometimes there are words. Sometimes there are not. As I've practiced the Way of Love, I find my prayer life and love for God have both deepened dramatically.

We seek freedom . . . from the many forces—sin, fear, oppression, and division—that pull us from living as God created us to be: dignified, whole, and free. (The Way of Love introductory brochure, part 1b)

The practice of *turn* is all about getting free. It is a revelation to hear leaders like Catherine Meeks talk about our work for racial justice, healing, and liberation in light of *turn*. Perhaps now we can speak more honestly about sin—one of those theological third rails few dare to go near—because we know this kind of truth-telling is a given for any who walk the road to freedom.

Go also has everything to do with freedom. Look at the dividing walls that separate us from one another, and the concrete walls that imprison too many people of color, poor people, refugees, and children. Those shackles are not God's will. Jesus opened doors, crossed borders, and moved into solidarity. When I see Episcopalians go to accompany asylum seekers on the border or to welcome refugees into their communities, I know it is part of God's dream that everyone might be free and knit into the one human family.

> *We seek abundant life . . . overflowing with joy, peace, generosity, and delight. Where there is enough for all because we all share with abandon. A life of meaning, given back to God and lived for others.* (The Way of Love introductory brochure, part 1c)

When we *bless*, we share our money, faith, time, possessions, gifts, and love. We trust abundance is real in our own lives and make abundant life and provision possible for others. Especially as we embrace evangelism—one of the primary ministries of blessing—we're sharing stories of the God who is a source of joy, peace, and delight to us. That brings more joy, peace, and delight into the world.

And oh yes, when I *rest* and pause with God, I can see the meaning and patterns that escaped my notice while I was running madly. I can see God's love written on the pages of my own life. I can hear the voices of ancestors who've walked this way before. I can be more intentional about what I eat, read, speak, and spend. The sweetness of life—even if it's just one sweet moment—only becomes real when I pause long enough to notice and give thanks for it.

Why the Way of Love? What difference does it make? Living these practices addresses and ultimately satisfies the most basic human longings: for love, for freedom, for abundant life. Life with Jesus really is more loving, more liberating, and more life-giving.

Give Me Jesus

As I write, it has been two years since Presiding Bishop Michael Curry gathered a strategic circle around him in December 2017 to reflect on the question: "How can I help our church to recenter our lives on Jesus of Nazareth?" If the Way of Love is making any difference in the life of our church, I hope it is that many Episcopalians are consciously, increasingly centered on the lively, sustaining presence of Jesus at the heart of our lives. We want more of Jesus.

The RenewalWorks group has surveyed more than 20,000 Episcopalians, and the vast majority of respondents identify as "troubled: restless or hungry for greater spiritual growth" or "complacent, low expectations of transformation and resistant to change and challenge."[2] Most have been in their churches for at least ten years. They came and/or stayed to meet the living God, and they remain open to that encounter, but for too many it's not happening.

---

2. RenewalWorks, "What We Are Learning," https://renewalworks.org/researchsummary, accessed May 13, 2020.

They've done what the church asked: attended worship, served on vestries and committees, run food pantries, tended the altar, repaired the building, given money, enjoyed fellowship. They're still waiting. Not for some flashy experience. Not to be entertained. They want to be more grounded and rooted in God and to feel their faith growing. They are hungry for Jesus, but don't know what to do with it.

I know their hunger. I've felt it for myself. It reminds me of Jesus and his words to the crowd: "I am the living bread that came down from heaven. Whoever eats this bread will live forever" (John 6:51). He knows how much people appreciated the bread and fish he provided for the five thousand on the mountain. Now he's trying to give them himself: his flesh, his blood, his very life. With this food, he promises, they will have life more abundant, richer and fuller than anything they could ever wrap their mind or tongue around.

If we say yes to that craving, and seek more of the God who is already seeking us, it makes all the difference. In his book *The God We Never Knew*, Marcus Borg cites a fascinating study. Among mainline churches—Episcopalians, Methodists, United Church of Christ, Lutherans, Presbyterians, and other historic denominations, rather than the newer Christian groups with roots in American soil—the ones that are growing are *full of God*.[3] There is a palpable sense that they are in love with God. They nurture a living, transforming, even risk-taking relationship with God. The churches that are declining

---

3. Marcus J. Borg, *The God We Never Knew: Beyond Dogmatic Religion to a More Authentic Contemporary Faith* (New York: HarperCollins, 1997).

are uncertain and hesitant about God, and unclear about their real need for or relationship with God.

There is good news here. Most Episcopalians are hungry for God. With the Way of Love, I hear us admitting that hunger and yearning and saying we want to do something about it. We're declaring, "God, you said you want us to abide in you. Well, here we come. We don't have all the answers, but we do have the hunger. Please, feed us."

So many of us yearn to be in authentic spiritual communities that grow love for God and for the world. With the Way of Love, we get to turn our collective energy to that hope, as a whole church. There is something powerful about admitting to this shared hunger and then taking up a shared commitment. It is as if this palpable spirit energy gets stirred and released. I know because everywhere I go, people volunteer that's what they are experiencing. Lifelong Episcopalians pull me aside to say, "I'm praying again. I thought I had forgotten how, but knowing we're all doing this together helped me to come back to it." People who never spoke much about Jesus are getting more and more comfortable talking about what it's like to follow and love him.

It's not that we were not following him before. I repeat: it is not that we were not following Jesus before the Way of Love. But when thousands of us step onto a path together—including a rule of life—how could it not make a difference?

There is no great mystery to what we have discovered here. Marjorie Thompson explains it well in her book *Soul Feast*. In it, she likens the spiritual life to a garden. Certain plants like tomatoes and beans need to attach to a structure of some kind in order to grow well. Without those supports, they would just collapse. And so it is with us:

> When it comes to spiritual growth, human beings are much like these plants. We need structure and support. Otherwise . . . the fruit of the Spirit in us gets tangled and is susceptible to corruption. . . . We need structure in order to have enough space, air, and light to flourish. Structure gives us the freedom to grow as we are meant to.
>
> There is a name in Christian tradition for the kind of structure that supports our spiritual growth. It is called a rule of life. A rule of life is a pattern of spiritual disciplines that provides structure and direction for growth in holiness. . . . It is meant to help us establish a rhythm of daily living, a basic order within which new freedoms can grow.[4]

Why the Way of Love? What difference does it make to be honest and vulnerable about our hunger for God and to seek intimacy with Jesus together and with intention? Now we can grow and thrive like those plants in need of a trellis or stake.

---

4. Marjorie Thompson, *Soul Feast: An Invitation to the Christian Spiritual Life* (Louisville, KY: Westminster John Knox Press, 2005), 145.

A Closing Prayer

Presiding Bishop Curry began by sharing his prayer for the Christian community and for individual Episcopalians and our churches. I close in like manner, with a prayer from H. Van der Looy's *Rule for a New Brother*:

> Following Jesus does not mean slavishly copying his life.
> It means making his choice of life your own,
> starting from your own potential
> and in the place where you find yourself.
> It means living for the values for which Jesus lived and died.
> . . . Amen.[5]

I say again, amen.

---

5. H. Van der Looy, *Rule for a New Brother* (Springfield, IL: Templegate Publishers, 1987), xx.

Contributors

The Rev. Megan Castellan is the rector of St. John's Episcopal Church in Ithaca, New York, and formerly the associate rector and chaplain of the Day School at St. Paul's, Kansas City, Missouri. Her writing is widely read in such online publications as *Episcopal Café*, *The Toast*, *McSweeney's*, and her own blog: *Red Shoes, Funny Shirt.* (Way of Love Practice: Bless)

Dr. Courtney Cowart is the executive director of the Society for the Increase of Ministry. She previously served as director of the Beecken Center and associate dean in the School of Theology of the University of the South in Sewanee, Tennessee. Cowart earned her doctorate from General Theological Seminary and has gained wide respect for her transformative ministries at Ground Zero and in New Orleans after Hurricane Katrina. She is the author of *An American Awakening: From Ground Zero to Katrina: The People We Are Free to Be.* (introductory chapter)

Michael Curry is the presiding bishop and primate of the Episcopal Church. Elected in 2015, he was previously bishop of the Diocese of North Carolina and a rector in Baltimore, Cincinnati, and Winston-Salem, North Carolina. He is the author of numerous books, including

The Power of Love, Following the Way of Jesus: Church's Teachings for a Changing World, and *Crazy Christians: A Call to Follow Jesus*. (foreword)

The Very Rev. Peter Elliott is a retired leader in the Anglican Church of Canada. He recently retired from his role as rector of Christ Church Cathedral and dean of New Westminster. Prior to coming to Vancouver, he was director of ministries in Church and Society for the Anglican Church of Canada. (Way of Love Practice: Rest)

The Rt. Rev. Frank Logue is the bishop of the Diocese of Georgia. He spent a decade as canon to the ordinary in the Diocese and before that founded King of Peace Episcopal Church. A member of the Executive Council of the Episcopal Church, Logue has nurtured church planting and renewal movements across the church. (Way of Love Practice: Worship)

The Rev. Dr. William Lupfer is the former rector of Trinity Church Wall Street in New York City. Before serving at Trinity, Dr. Lupfer was dean of Trinity Episcopal Cathedral in Portland, Oregon. A former campus minister and prison chaplain, he completed doctoral study on the intersection of parish leadership and spiritual formation. (Way of Love Practice: Rest)

Dr. Catherine Meeks is executive director of the Absalom Jones Center for Racial Healing in Atlanta and the editor of *Living into God's Dream: Dismantling Racism in America*. Dr. Meeks is a key leader at the intersection of spiritual formation and justice, and is the retired Clara Carter Acree Distinguished Professor of Socio-Cultural Studies from Wesleyan College. (Way of Love Practice: Turn)

The Rev. Canon Jesús Reyes is the canon for congregational development in the Diocese of El Camino Real (Central California). He nurtures mission and multicultural development in congregations at the diocesan and church-wide levels. Prior to serving in El Camino Real, Reyes planted Santa Maria Episcopal Church in Falls Church, Virginia, and ministered extensively in Mexico and Brazil. (Rule of Life)

The Rev. Canon Stephanie Spellers serves as canon to the presiding bishop for evangelism, reconciliation, and care of creation. The author of *Radical Welcome: Embracing God, The Other and the Spirit of Transformation* and *The Episcopal Way* (with Eric Law), she has worked at General Theological Seminary and in the Diocese of Long Island; founded The Crossing ministry within St. Paul's Cathedral in Boston; and served as chaplain to the Episcopal Church's House of Bishops and as an editor for Church Publishing. (concluding chapter)

Brother David Vryhof is an Episcopal priest and member of the Society of St. John the Evangelist, a religious order based in Cambridge, Massachusetts. He serves as the order's assistant superior and oversees its popular communications, including www.catchthe life.org and "Brother, Give Us a Word," a daily e-mail offering from the Brothers. (Way of Love Practice: Pray)

The Rt. Rev. Robert Wright is the bishop of the Diocese of Atlanta. He has also served as rector of St. Paul's Episcopal Church in Atlanta, as a school chaplain, and on the staff of the Cathedral of St. John the Divine in New York City. He is the coauthor with Donna Mote of *The Go Guide*, a book of practical tips for following Jesus into the world. (Way of Love Practice: Go)

The Rev. Dr. Dwight Zscheile is the vice president of innovation and associate professor of Congregational Mission and Leadership at Luther Seminary in St. Paul, Minnesota. The author of *The Agile Church: Spirit-Led Innovation in an Uncertain Age* and *People of the Way: Renewing Episcopal Identity*, Zscheile serves part time as associate priest at St. Matthew's Episcopal Church. (Way of Love Practice: Learn)

Printed in the USA
CPSIA information can be obtained
at www.ICGtesting.com
JSHW012053140824
68134JS00035B/3418

9 781640 652965